THE
JOURNEY
FROM
PAIN TO
Purpose

Charlyn Singleton

THE JOURNEY FROM PAIN TO PURPOSE
ISBN 1-880809-46-X
Printed in the United States of America
Copyright © 2005 by Charlyn Singleton

Legacy Publishers International
1301 South Clinton Street
Denver, CO 80247
Phone: 303-283-7480 FAX: 303-283-7536

Library of Congress Cataloging-in-Publication Data Pending

Dedication

This book is lovingly dedicated:

First, to my Savior and Lord Jesus Christ: You are my reason for living. I love You with all my heart, mind, and soul.

To my husband, Pastor Chuck Singleton: I thank you for being my blessing from God. I know God loves me because He gave you to me. It has been an honor to walk beside you in life, and I pray that we have the privilege to grow old together.

To my sons, Chuck, Chris, Corey, and Cary: You are my greatest joy from God.

To my mother, Clotiel Palmer: You have been my greatest cheerleader throughout life. Whether welcomed or not, you have pushed me to become all God has purposed me for. Thank you for your love of life. You are the epitome of a great woman of God and an awesome mother. Although Daddy has gone on to be with the Lord, I thank you both for raising me in church, teaching me not to look at the size of any obstacle, and for pouring into me a spirit of excellence.

To those who helped me with the book: To my sister, Gloria Palmer-Dunlap: You have been my greatest support as I have written this book. To Karen Jones: You are the best friend anyone could have. To Linda Cumberland: You started the project with me and stayed with me to the end. To all of you: Thank you for the countless hours reading and re-reading, and for all the late hours we spent correcting the manuscript. To Phyllis Robinson: You encouraged me to take the first step, which was half the journey. I will forever be in your debt.

Acknowledgements

I gratefully acknowledge the following:

My little sister, Dianna Litt: You have been such a joy and support to me. My brother, Eugene (Joseph) Palmer: You are the best brother anyone could have.

My spiritual daughters, Donna Michelle Hope, and LaShon Tilmon: Although I was not blessed to birth daughters, God filled that desire in my heart through you.

My spiritual mother, Marie Brewington: Thank you for your countless prayers and counsel.

The staff of God's Woman Conferences: You are the most wonderful staff any ministry leader could hope to have. Vera Williams and Becky Davis: Thank you for running the office while I spent so many hours on this book.

My in-laws, Pastor Isaac and Pearl Singleton: Thank for loving me as if you were my blood parents.

My Uncle, George Palmer and all my friends and relatives in Donora, Pennsylvania: All the wonderful memories of growing up in Donora will forever fill my thoughts.

The members of Loveland Church: Thank you for supporting me these thirty years.

Finally, my editor, Harold McDougal and his wife Andy: Thank you, Harold, for helping me to envision this book. And thank you, Andy. Your words of encouragement right from the beginning of the project were a source of inspiration to me.

Contents

Introduction

As a teacher of the Word of God now for many years, I have often felt that I didn't have much to say to people, but that God's Word always had something to say. In fact, it has everything to say. If we can assimilate what God has said to us in His Word and make it part of our daily lives, it will change both our present and our future.

The particular passage upon which the message of this book is based first ministered powerfully to my own soul, and because I had been blessed by it, I knew that others would be blessed too. So I began teaching it, and this book is the result.

In some ways, the story of Joseph is an old one. Many of us have heard it from the time we were small children, and it has inspired many generations. But I found that it was not old in relevance. It may be that we have heard his story so much that we think we have nothing else to learn from it, but I promise you that's not the case. This story is relevant to life in the twenty-first century.

Joseph teaches us many things. Among them is the powerful fact that life is a mixture of joys and sufferings, but we can rejoice in them both, for they are both for our good. Another truth we learn from his life is that things seem to come to us in seasons. We may experience a season of joy and then a season of suffering and later another season of joy and another season of suffering. Or the suffering may come first, and then the joy. God chooses our seasons for His own purposes.

Sometimes it seems hard to see God in all of this. Where is He? What is He doing? Has He forgotten us? As we learn what the Word of God teaches us, it will keep us steady through these inevitable times of questioning.

"Does the Lord see me?" "Does He hear my cry?" "Does He see my tears?" Of course He does, but that isn't always apparent in the moment. Sometimes our trials are so great that they seem to obscure everything else about life. And, at times, it seems that we are very much alone.

This was all true for Joseph, who, as a very young man, was mistreated, rejected, falsely accused, and abused. He was even imprisoned on false charges and had to stay in prison without recourse for years. There was no one on whom he could call for help.

But through all of this, Joseph learned to hold on to God, even when he couldn't see Him, and even when circumstances made it look as if God had abandoned him. The end result was that God exalted Joseph into his destiny, his true purpose in life, that for which He had been preparing Joseph all along.

Although it is sometimes difficult for us to believe, God uses all of the events of our lives to prepare us for the future. This is important to those who are desirous of accomplishing great things in life, but who have not yet realized that on your journey to purpose you may encounter pain and suffering.

Most people see only the glory of position and accomplishment, and immediately they want to be involved with the place of glory. Often, however, they fail to realize that the place of glory is only to be found in the specific place of purpose. And to get to the place of specific purpose we must go through the place of pain. I don't know anyone who has found their specific place of purpose without first experiencing at least one season of pain. And most, like Joseph, have experienced many such seasons.

There are times in life when God speaks a word to you, but the facts of your life and/or your current circumstances, just don't match your faith and your revelation. In those moments, we must depend on the promises of the Word of God and know that God has a purpose in it all.

I appreciate that Joseph and other Bible characters suffered even as we do today. That shows us that we're not alone. What we have come to call "Bible characters" were real people who experienced real life situations, just like you and me. And because they overcame, we can also overcome. The fact that Joseph suffered for his faith makes me to know that I can endure anything that might come my way.

Introduction

Come with me now, as we explore together more fully the amazing story of Joseph and begin to understand the times *When Purpose Includes Pain.*

Charlyn Singleton
Upland, California

—»‑•‑«—

CHAPTER 1

Purpose, Plans, and Destiny

I waited for a response, but instead heard only silence. Finally, in a barely audible voice, I heard a sigh and these words, "Well … he lived … and died … and nothing in between." I will never forget those sentiments my mother voiced a few years ago. A very close friend of the family had died, and this was about all she could think to say about him.

Much earlier in life, this friend had suffered the tragic loss of love and had, as a result, given up on life. Even though I was just a child at the time, I still remembered hearing about that breakup. It had left him reeling. And, although the man kept living in the flesh, a part of his soul had died that year.

With that loss, came a loss of purpose, and this friend of the family ended up simply marking time until his tragic death so many years later.

What A Waste!

Every time I heard the popular television ad from the college scholarship fund, "A mind is a terrible thing to waste," I thought of him. The slogan was all too true. A wasted purpose is just as tragic, yet we see it all the time. People of every age group fail to live up to their potential, and thus, are not able to fulfill their purpose in life.

It happens for whatever reason. Sometimes it's pain and disappointment, sometimes premature death, sometimes lack of focus, sometimes lack of motivation. Whatever the reasons, too many people end up marking time until death overtakes them.

Although there are a myriad of reasons that purpose goes unfulfilled, everyone on this earth has a purpose. There are no exceptions to that rule. This means that you and everyone you know are here for a specific reason. I personally believe that, deep down, most people instinctively know this and want their lives to count for something.

Take a Picture of Me!

At Christmas, my niece and nephews seemed to follow the cameras around the celebrations at our house. People love to get into pictures. Pick up a camera and start taking pictures, and notice how people will suddenly gather around you. Some may stand back, as if they're not all that interested, but even these seem to be watching out of the corner of their eye.

Some timid ones will hang back, hoping to be invited to get into the picture, but the bolder ones will either express a desire to be in the picture or simply join the group without any fanfare. "I want to be in the picture!" some of them will shout.

I'm sure you have experienced this, and this is the reason that many times, while taking pictures, you will end up taking a picture of someone you didn't really want in the picture.

Have you ever looked at family photos, and there in the picture you see someone who was not even related to the others. They just wanted to be in the picture. And, because they knew someone in the family or had some relationship to them, they end up in the picture (much to the chagrin of the real family members, who didn't have the heart or courage to ask them to stand aside).

Yes, people love to take pictures, and this has absolutely nothing to do with good looks. Unattractive people enjoy taking pictures as much as gorgeous ones do. Did you ever wonder about this? Perhaps even this unusual behavior is linked to purpose.

When you think about it, a photo is a lasting image of a person. It's something that preserves their memory, a proof, of sorts, that they were there.

And most of us have an innate desire to be remembered. It's for this reason that such great amounts of money are spent on tombstones. There is recorded the name, the date of birth, the date of death and sometimes other facts. In other words, this person was here.

Wasted Years

All this can be tied to purpose. Yes, we're here, and we want our life to count. We want to live a life that matters.

The problem comes with discovering that purpose. Many people would love to fulfill their purpose … if they only knew what it was. But finding purpose can be just as frustrating as deciding that we want to get closer to God.

The desire is there, and we know that we should study the Bible, His Holy Word. But where do we begin? Do we read first the Old Testament or the New Testament? Which book should we start with? Which chapter should we read? Many times, because of this dilemma of not knowing how to get started, we don't start at all, and our original commitment fades with time.

For years, I wanted to write a book. I knew that I was born to write, and yet every time I really got serious about writing, I couldn't decide what to write about. There were so many important subjects. In the end, because I couldn't settle on an appropriate subject, I lost interest and moved on to something else. Still, in the back of my mind, was that ever-present gnawing that told me that I was supposed to write books.

Can you guess what my problem was? I didn't want to write just any old book. I wanted to write a book that everyone—black, brown, or white, male or female, young or old—would be interested in. It would have to be a best-selling book, because, in my heart, I didn't want to be a failure. This desire for great success coupled with an underlying fear of failure became an enemy to my purpose.

There's an old adage that goes like this: "It's a cinch by the inch, but a trial by the mile." Taking the first step is always half of the battle.

The answer to the dilemma, of course, is to do *something*. It might not gain much attention, it might benefit only a few, and you might not become famous by doing it, but at least you'll be accomplishing something with the precious life God has given you. Something is always better than nothing. Something is a beginning, movement toward a more complete destiny.

One day it finally dawned on me that I was wasting valuable years trying to write for everyone. If I didn't get started doing what God had purposed me for, one day I would look back and greatly regret having wasted many years of my life.

When "Great" Becomes the Enemy of "Important"

I'm not alone in this, by any stretch of the imagination. Many of us, because we want to be great, sometimes end up missing the important opportunities along the way.

Think about it. One person has a deep desire to become a great athlete, another desires to become a great entertainer, and another desires to become an important politician. Many of us have a deep desire to become wealthy. Those who fail to achieve their desire, and a majority of us do, are not hindered by a lack of intelligence or ability. More often we fail to accomplish our purpose because we're only motivated toward greatness, and don't know the steps necessary to get us there.

This explains why young people can memorize the lines of many popular songs, but they can't seem to remember basic multiplication. There's no glory in doing math. But imagine yourself on stage in front of thousands of adoring fans, and that's powerful motivation.

That's real glory, real success, and we all want to be at the top of our field, at the top of whatever is important to us. We want to be celebrated. But greatness never comes overnight, and it never comes without a price.

The amusing paradox is this: If we do the little things that come our way and do them well (even though they may not get a lot of attention), they can all add up to cause us to fulfill our purpose, making us great, and giving other people something to remember us by—all at the same time.

Take, for instance, the high school football player who wants to someday star in the NFL. He can hold onto that dream for stardom and, at the same time, focus on his current responsibilities—making good grades in high school. If he does well, he may get a scholarship to college. There he can work toward earning a degree.

Life is not like playing hopscotch. You can't just hop your way to overnight success.

He plays college football and does fairly well, but still he's not selected to play in the pros. This could be the end of his life, or it could be the beginning of an even better one.

During those years in college, it may dawn on him that he has a natural ability for law. He can then go on to study law, become a lawyer, practice law, and eventually become a partner or start his own firm. If, on the other hand, he allows his failure to make it to pro football discourage him and cause him to quit trying, he may end up on the unemployment roles or even become a criminal. We cannot allow dreams of greatness to keep us from important current achievements, or we will never discover our purpose in life and prosper.

It's okay to dream and to dream big, but until that dream becomes reality, we have to go on accomplishing in the smaller day-to-day matters of life.

Traveling Eighty Miles to Preach to Three People

There's absolutely nothing wrong with wanting to be at the top of your field (when yours is an honest profession), but don't expect to get to the top overnight. Life is not like playing hopscotch. You can't just hop your way to overnight success.

Sometimes it seems to us that others have done just that. Yesterday, we had no idea who a particular person was, and now, seemingly overnight, everyone knows his or her name. But that's probably misleading. What most likely happened is that the person in question was working behind the scenes for quite some time before we heard of them.

A few years ago, I was watching the "Praise the Lord" show on the Trinity Broadcasting Network. Noted preacher, T.D. Jakes, was on that night. While talking about his life growing up, he said that he had never learned to ride a bicycle, and he had never gone to a football or basketball game while attending high school. His father had gotten very ill, when T.D. was just a young child, and so he had spent his childhood and teenage years helping his mother care for his Dad.

He went on to say something like this: "People think that I just started preaching because they just started hearing about me. They see the fame, and they hear me now preaching to the masses, but what they fail to realize is that I've been preaching for over twenty-five years.

"I can remember driving miles to preach in small country churches. One time I drove eighty miles to preach to three people, and two of them went to sleep."

I appreciated that statement when I first heard it some years ago, and I still appreciate it today. Most people can't see the years of hard work, sacrifice, and pain behind the glory when others rise to the top, but I can guarantee you that it's there. You simply don't get to the place of purpose without first going through the place of pain.

"I Was Born to Coach"

"I was born to coach." As I flipped through the channels of my television one night, I heard a man make this statement. I paused for a moment to hear more. The man was Coach Ken Carter, former coach of the undefeated Richmond High basketball team (Richmond, California). Coach Carter is celebrated for locking out his state-playoff-bound varsity basketball team from the gym because of poor academic performance.

The interview that night was about the soon-to-be-released movie about his life. The coach spoke about how as a young child he had told his mother that one day they were going to make a movie about him. When it happened, he told her, he would buy her a house.

As a boy Ken Carter saw himself accomplishing some great purpose that would be worthy of a biographical movie about him. But when he locked his players out of the gym, I really don't think he had a movie deal in mind. No, at that moment he was practicing the important. He was teaching his players that being average was just not good enough.

Although some praised him for this valiant act, he suffered the staunch criticism of the student body, many parents, and most of the school board. Yet, because he did not allow that opposition to stop him, because he did not allow the great to become the enemy of the important, audiences throughout the world will be blessed by his story.

At this time in his life, Coach Ken Carter is accomplishing his childhood dream of greatness. And to know, at such a young age, that you want to accomplish something great in your life is wonderful.

Some can identify with Coach Carter's experience. As a child, you dreamed of great plans and destinies for yourself. You may remember the day you graduated. You were determined to go out and make your mark on the world. Or perhaps you intended to meet your knight in shining armor and live happily ever after. Whatever the case, you saw yourself doing something great. At the very least, you hoped your life would be a good one.

Then, as you began to experience the realities of life, your bubble burst. You found that life is not just filled with good. There is plenty of bad to go around: in business, marriage, or any other endeavor. You found that life could bring much pain, much disappointment, much pressure, and much monotony.

Still, deep down, that dream you had in high school lingers in your heart. Even on the days you simply go through the motions of life, you know there's more.

The Motions of Life

You may have been so wounded by life that you've settled for less than your dream. As a consequence, you may be like our family friend, only marking time until death because a part of your soul has already died. Someone or something of some circumstance broke your heart and left you for dead. But it's time to get up, and it's time to go back to the place you buried your dream. Dig it up, wipe it off, and remember what you once longed for.

No matter what you've gone through or are presently going through, God has a purpose, plan, and destiny for you. It's okay that you were disappointed or even devastated. It's even okay that you walked away from the dream, from life, and from everything else that mattered. God will use even that, as you go through your various places of purpose to your final destiny. The wonderful thing about purpose is that God uses *everything,* even our worst and our most painful times, to prepare us for that purpose.

Because we sometimes don't understand this, in the midst of our pain and disappointment, we often forget about purpose and lay our dreams down. People, situations, and circumstances take their toll on us physically, mentally, emotionally, and psychologically. And when this happens, it seems that purpose is just too difficult to achieve.

If we could understand how the negative things we face in life affect our destiny, we would be more content, patient, peaceful—and even thankful. Understanding is a powerful therapist. This is one of the reasons the Bible tells us to *"get understanding"* (Proverbs 4:5 and 7) .

The Power of Understanding

A few years ago I broke out in hives all over my body. It started one morning with hives on my feet and my lower legs. Then, over the next few days, the hives worked their way up my body. Finally, they hit my face, and I became alarmed and sought medical attention. Still, the hives did not get better; they only grew worse. And the itching associated with them was severe.

Before it was over, I had visited three different doctors. One of them told me that I needed an operation to open up my unusually small nostrils. I wasn't very happy when I left his office. I didn't care about my nostrils; I needed someone to give me something to get rid of the hives.

Finally, my friend LeNell Roussell told me that I should visit Dr. Laurie Woll, a dermatologist she knew. When Dr. Woll stepped into her office, she asked me a couple of questions about my life and my family. She then looked at me and gave me a quick diagnosis: "Your hives are caused by stress."

"But I'm not under any stress," I objected. "My life is good."

She told me I needed to understand that *life itself is stressful.* In my case, I was juggling the responsibilities of a young pastor's wife, while at the same time being a mother to four young children ranging in ages from five to twelve. I was often on the road teaching, and, on top of all that, I was heading up my own ministry. That was enough stress for anyone, she assured me, handing me a ten-day prescription for something she felt would help alleviate the symptoms.

As I left Dr. Woll's office that day, in spite of the fact that I was still covered from head to toe with hives, I felt wonderful. In fact, I was walking on air. This really would not make sense without understanding that although I left Dr. Woll's office with only a prescription in my hand, I now had something more powerful in my heart—an understanding of what was happening to me. That understanding was precious, for it allowed me to look past the outer evidence of the present hives to the future. I now knew that, in time, they would pass.

When you have inner understanding, it takes precedence over your outer circumstances.

When you have inner understanding, it takes precedence over your outer circumstances. In the same way, if you can come to understand that your present situation can eventually change and that life's good times and delays are just training for your purpose, not only will your outer conduct be remarkably bettered, but you will become an effective witness to the power of understanding.

The Process of Purpose

We first need to understand that there's a difference between purpose and destiny. Succinctly speaking, destiny implies just that—a destination, a future expectation. But *purpose is a process that takes place as we journey through life.* It's so important that we get this into our hearts and keep it ever before us. This one truth will get you through just about anything and everything in life. If you realize that whatever you're going through is part of your purpose, you can keep going.

Your successes are part of your purpose, and your failures are part of your purpose. People who are with you are part of God's plan for your purpose, and negative, backbiting people, who seem to be on assignment from hell and continually stand against you, are also part of your purpose.

Why do I say this? Because we have God's promise that *"all things work together for good"* (Romans 8:28). Not all things are good, and if someone tries

9

to tell you they are, then there's something terribly wrong with them. It is not a good thing when people suffer loss, death, or misfortune. Yet, even though all things are not good, God says that *"all things work together for good."*

Let me give you an example of this. If you eat flour by itself, it's not good. If you eat sugar by itself, it's not good. If you eat baking powder by itself, it's not good. If you eat butter by itself, it's not good. If you eat salt by itself, it's not good. If you eat vanilla flavor by itself, it's not good. If you drink oil by itself, it's not good. Some even say that if you drink milk by itself, it's not good. But if you put them all together, you get a cake that's good. That's how purpose works.

With Great Purpose Comes Great Pain

When you think about it, purpose is never easy. Yet, everybody wants to get to the place of purpose. The problem comes when we want to get there with as little pain and inconvenience as possible. This is why so many people will never experience that which they are purposed and destined for.

On your journey to purpose you will always encounter pain, disappointment, and delays. Purpose takes much patience, faith, and overcoming. But stay in the fight, for with great purpose comes great accomplishment. With fulfilled purpose also comes great satisfaction.

If you're one of those who want to live a life of purpose, but don't understand why purpose is so hard or takes so long, this book will be an informative journey for you. You were born to be something. Sometimes, all we need is a little insight, first, to inform, and then to encourage us to get there. But keep in mind: if you want your life to make a difference on this earth, you will experience pain.

I can think of no better example of this than the story of Joseph in the Bible. Whether you're a Christian or not, a churchgoer or not, I guarantee you that Joseph's story will help put everything that has happened to you up to this point in your in life in perspective. His story shows you how people and circumstances that come against you can actually help you in your quest for purpose. His story gives insight on the times in life when you experience setbacks or find your life on hold. Finally, his story shows that purpose is a journey that often takes time to complete, it leads you through numerous unexpected events, and it ushers you into unfamiliar, even hostile, places.

And yet, Joseph's story also shows that God is always in control. It shows that when God destines you for greatness, no man can stop you. Finally, his story shows us, that although there is a time that we're required to go through seasons of suffering, there is always a time for us to come out of them. We will not stay in that season forever.

Joseph was a man of great purpose ordained by God. But great purpose will always include great pain. Let's look at his story.

—»·•·«—

CHAPTER 2

Your Family and Purpose

Now Israel [Jacob] loved Joseph more than all his children, because he was
the son of his old age: and he made him a coat of many colours.

Genesis 37:3

The story of Joseph centers around his coat of many colors. The day Jacob gave him that coat was probably a day of great joy for the boy, but it was not so for the family as a whole. Joseph had ten brothers, and they were not thrilled with this special gift given to their little brother. Their father (and circumstances) had planted negative seeds in them earlier in life, and seeing their father lovingly give Joseph that coat only further watered and nurtured those seeds. But unbeknownst to Jacob, Joseph, and the brothers, that coat would eventually change all of their lives and destinies.

The story is a fascinating one, but to understand the significance of Joseph's famous coat, we must first go back and gain an understanding of his family history.

A Generational Problem

The significant point to note about this family is that it was suffering from a generational problem of sibling rivalry. The sins of the fathers were being visited upon the children.

Have you ever noticed that certain characteristics and actions, no matter how wrong, seem to run in families? Daddy beat Mama and now Jr. beats his wife. Mama had three children out of wedlock, and now daughter has three children by three different men. Daddy had a mistress on the side, and now son lives with his girlfriend. Parents did not go to church, and now the children don't go to church either. These are cycles of behavior that run in families.

...when wrong behavior is practiced in a family, the children often don't recognize that behavior for what it is: wrong.

Why is this? Are certain families just destined to repeat negative, destructive behavior? I believe it comes down to the concept of the sins of the father being visited upon future generations. It's not as if God puts a curse on children, to punish them for wrongs their fathers have done. No! The fathers, in essence, bring down the curse upon themselves.

You see, when wrong behavior is practiced in a family, the children often don't recognize that behavior for what it is: wrong. Instead, because the children see their parents practicing certain behavior, they grow up thinking that behavior is acceptable. And, because the behavior is considered acceptable, the children grow to practice it themselves. Their children, in turn, will do the same thing. And, in time, this produces a family flaw.

This is where racism comes from, and it is also at the root of discrimination. This is why daddy had a foul mouth, and now most of his children have foul mouths. Daddy was an alcoholic, and now son is a drug addict. Because their parents didn't think that a better life was obtainable, their children often mark time, passing through a life in disillusionment, moving from one minimum-wage job to another. Children practice what they see, not what they're told. This can lead to generational curses.

In a moment, we'll see this repeated behavior in Abraham's family and the generational problem it led to. This was at the root of Joseph's pain and also his purpose.

God's Covenant with Abraham

Joseph was the great-grandson of the patriarch Abraham. To understand Joseph more fully, we must understand something of God's unique dealings with Abraham, his son Isaac, and his son Jacob.

Many years before Joseph's times, God called Abraham to leave his land and his people and to go to a place where he could form a new nation, a nation that would be free of idolatry. It was to be a nation that would present an example for all other nations of the earth to follow and a nation through whom the Messiah, the Savior of all mankind, would be born.

Having received the initial call for this adventure, Abraham embarked on a journey of faith that would take many years and eventually lead him to settle in the land of Canaan. In Canaan, God made a covenant, or promise, with Abraham.

Through that covenant, God told Abraham that he would be blessed, that his children would be blessed, and that his children's children would be blessed. This blessing would continue on down to other generations. God said that He would give Abraham and his descendants the land of Canaan as an everlasting possession, that He would greatly multiply Abraham's seed, and that through him and his descendants all the nations of the earth would be blessed.

With this as a backdrop for this story, we will begin to trace the generational problems in this family. The first generation to suffer hate and conflict was that of Ishmael and Isaac, the sons of Abraham. When God made His covenant to multiply Abraham's seed, Abraham was already seventy-five, but he still had no children. This was because his wife Sarah was barren.

Time passed and Abraham didn't have the many sons God had promised him. In reality, he had failed to have even one son. Still, God had told him that his descendants would eventually bless all of mankind.

This was trying for Abraham. He could not understand the delay in the heavenlies. The continual passing of time seemed to dispute God's word, and impatience set in. After years of waiting for their promised son to be born, Sarah, Abraham's wife, came up with a suggestion of how they could resolve this crisis. They would help God. Thinking that she was unable to bear children, she suggested that he have a child by Hagar, her servant girl.

15

We must understand the culture of the time to fully appreciate this act of desperation on Sarah's part. In ancient times, if a wife was unable to bear children, it was permissible under existing law (man's law, not God's) for the man to sire children by his wife's servant. The servant then became a lesser wife, one commonly known as a concubine. Although a concubine bore a child for her master, that child was, in actuality, considered to be the child of the man's wife.

Timing in the Heavenlies

How could Sarah have done such a thing? Why would she give her husband another woman? Well, it may seem logical to question Sarah's actions, but we will have to admit she was not alone. People often try to help God, when it seems that He's late.

I'm reminded of a magazine interview I gave a few years ago. The reporter asked me this question. "What is the greatest hindrance to the Christian life?" I immediately answered, "Trials."

Then I paused, and pondered the question a little more in depth. "There are two equal hindrances to living the Christian life," I said. "They are trials and time."

Because we often don't understand God's eternal timetable, we don't understand that there's timing in the heavenlies for answered prayer. When we pray a prayer, we always want the answer now. And when we have a need, we want the answer yesterday. But it doesn't work that way.

There are times when God gives us a word, some promise in our heart of something He's going to do for us or through us. When that promise becomes fixed in our heart, we begin—in faith—to wait for it. But, as time passes and the answer doesn't come, we begin to think that God is late. During this time, if our situation has become extremely painful or disappointing, this can cause great discouragement and eventually lead to wrongful behavior, as was the case with Sarah.

Take the marriage that's currently going through a season of suffering. We pray ... and pray ... and pray. We speak words of faith: "God is able. God is the God of the impossible. God is El Roi, the God who sees." We go to church and sing songs of encouragement: "He's Able, Learn How to Trust in Jesus," "Peace Be Still." "Whenever the Lord says peace, there will be peace," we sing. We tell ourselves that we can hold on and wait.

But as more time passes, the songs no longer encourage us, and the words of faith seem empty. Then, because we feel that the period of waiting needs to be over, we take matters into our own hands. We figure out our own solutions and then act upon them.

Many divorces result from our not understanding timing in the heavenlies, and this is also the reason many marry the wrong person. This is where bitterness comes from, and it's why many people give up. But God's timing is everything. The old folks among us used to have a saying: "HE may not come when you want Him to, but He's always on time."

In actuality, this saying speaks of timing in the heavenlies. Let me encourage you. Hold on! Hang on! Don't give up! And don't take matters into your own hands! God is the God of answered prayers—not you.

Also, just because God has not moved on your behalf up to now does not mean that the situation or circumstance will always be that way. If Sarah had known this truth, she would have saved herself much heartache.

The Consequences of "Helping God"

As always, when we "help God," there are negative consequences. In the case of Sarah and Abraham, a major problem arose after Hagar conceived and bore Abraham a son, whom he named Ishmael. Hagar got uppity and started looking down on Sarah, as though she were nothing. After all, Hagar had borne Abraham his precious promised son (or so she thought). As a result, Sarah now hated Hagar and started being abusive to her.

How dare Hagar look down on her as if she were nothing! After all, Abraham was *her* husband. Hagar was nothing more that a servant, a slave. Sarah would show her who she was "messing" with.

Eventually Hagar could stand the abuse no more. She took her baby and ran away. But God sent an angel and told her, much to her dismay (and Sarah's), to go back home.

The Spirit of Hagar

Allow me to make an observation here. There are many Hagars in the world. These are women who have the man, but not the name. These women, like Hagar, look down on the wife—as if she were nothing. After all, why does the man need his wife when he has *her*? You can see this in movies, and you can also see it in the real world.

The Hagars of this world roll their eyes at the wife, and either ignore or talk negatively about his wife. This is not to say that they are always sexually involved with the man. They may not be having a physical affair at all. Often, it's an emotional involvement, an affair of the heart.

Many times the man is oblivious to this fact. You see, Hagar may just like being closely aligned with the man. She may just want too much of his favor. This is why women bake cakes and cook favorite dishes for their pastor, while they completely ignore, don't like, and resent his wife. At home, they pay little attention to their own husbands and feed them TV dinners.

These women want to be special to the pastor, and they want to be seen by the congregation as special to him. They don't know that the spirit of Hagar rests on them.

Later in the story, when Hagar actually left, she and Ishmael found themselves once again alone in the wilderness. This proved to be too much for Hagar, and eventually she and her son fell victim to that wilderness. They were about to die from thirst, when Hagar decided that they should pray. It is most interesting what the Bible says about this: God heard and sent an angel, but it was in response to the boy's prayers—not Hagar's.

Over the years, Hagar's attitude did not change, and God doesn't bless "mess." So He didn't hear her prayers. If you're a Hagar in any sense of the word, and you're mistreating a man's wife, you're being a hindrance to your own prayers. Don't expect God to answer you as long as you remain in this sorry state.

When God Gives a Word

Fifteen years after Ishmael was born, Sarah finally conceived and gave birth to Isaac at the ripe old age of ninety. God had given a word: Sarah would bear Abraham a son. Neither Sarah's age, nor Abraham's age was at issue. It didn't matter that they were both well past child bearing age. God had spoken a word about their destiny, and if He had to revive both of their bodies to fulfill that word, then He would do it. After all, He's *"the resurrection and the life"* (John 11:25).

In the same way, if God has given you a word, it's never too late for that word to come to pass. No matter what the situation or circumstance, no matter how late it looks, always remember that God is able.

The Consequence of Choice

Sarah conceived and gave birth to Isaac, but the two sons were never at peace with each other. When Isaac was still just a toddler, one day Sarah saw the now-teenaged Ishmael mistreating her beloved son, and that was it. Hagar had to go.

Sarah voiced this to Abraham, demanding, "Get rid of this slave woman and her son." This pained Abraham deeply. Ishmael was his son too, and he loved him dearly.

But God spoke to Abraham to do as Sarah had said. His promised descendants would come through Isaac. He would also bless Ishmael and make him a great nation, but Isaac was the recipient of the covenant. Remember, God had made a covenant with Abraham, to give him and his descendants the land of Canaan, and to bless all the earth through those descendants. That promise would be fulfilled through Isaac and his seed, with whom God chose to renew the covenant.

Even though God gave a clear word on Isaac being the carrier and inheritor of the promise, there was still the matter of consequence. There are always consequences associated with any choice. To this day, as a consequence of Sarah's choice to give Abraham her servant Hagar, the strife between Isaac and Ishmael continues. The two still vie for supremacy. Today's headlines are continually filled with the strife in the Middle East between the Jews (children of Isaac) and the Arabs (children of Ishmael). It all started with their forefathers' struggle.

When Joseph's brothers stripped him of his coat of many colors, they were the third generation of strife. The second generation to suffer the strife between brothers had been that of Jacob and Esau, the sons of Isaac.

The Case of Rebekah

As I noted earlier, Abraham sent Hagar and Ishmael away, because Isaac was to be the carrier of God's promise to him. Then, Sarah died, and suddenly all of Abraham's attention was focused on his beloved Isaac. Apprehensive that Isaac would marry one of the pagan Canaanite women, Abraham sent his servant Eliezer to his homeland to seek a bride for his son among his relatives.

Setting out on the journey, Eliezer eventually came to Padan-Aram, where Abraham's people lived. Upon arriving there, God blessed Eliezer's loyalty and miraculously led him to Rebekah, who was Abraham's brother Nahor's granddaughter. To put it more clearly, she was Abraham's great niece. She accepted his proposal of marriage to Isaac and set off with Eliezer for the return trip.

After many months on the back of camels, Eliezer, Rebekah, and the rest of the caravan arrived in the land of Canaan. There, she and Isaac were married, and waited expectantly for their first child. But, as in the case of Abraham and Sarah, this couple too had to wait many years for a child. In fact, Rebekah and Isaac had been married for twenty years before God finally answered their prayers. Then, again, God blessed them, not just with one son, but with two, twins—Jacob and Esau.

Fighting in the Womb

There had been a strong sibling rivalry between Isaac and Ishmael, and the same could be said of the sons of Isaac and Rebekah. This time however, the struggle started early—in the womb.

When Rebekah finally became pregnant, it seemed to her as if there was a fight going on inside of her. This caused her so much pain that she prayed to God about it. He revealed to her that she was having twins, each of whom would grow to be great nations. He also told her that these two brothers would struggle, and, what seems the most important point to remember in all this, that the older would serve the younger.

On the day the twins were born, out came Esau first, completely covered with hair. Then, with his hand grabbing Esau's heel, out came Jacob.

These two brothers were as different as any two brothers could be. Esau was free-spirited, independent, and adventuresome. Jacob, on the other hand, was a quiet, meditative man. Esau grew up to be an expert hunter, an out-doorsman. Jacob, again quite the opposite, preferred life at home. He was an indoorsman. And now, let the games begin.

An Undetected Weakness, An Unexpected Opportunity

The boys grew to be men. One day Esau came to Jacob's tent, literally "wiped out" from a long day outdoors. Esau was tired and he was hungry. Indoorsman Jacob had made a pot of stew, of which Esau desperately wanted some. What happened next seems to show that Jacob and Esau were void of brotherly love. Instead of feeling compassion for his starving, tired brother and just giving him some nourishment for his tired body, the wheels of Jacob's mind went into action. He decided that he would sell the stew to Esau for his rights as the first-born son.

Because Esau was tired and hungry, a birthright at that moment in time didn't seem to be any good to him, so he hastily agreed. But Jacob needed more. *"First, swear to me,"* he insisted (Genesis 25:33), and Esau did it. Jacob gave him the stew and some bread, and Esau ate them and then left.

Jacob had obviously been inwardly desirous of Esau's birthright for some time before this incident. This seems to be the only way to explain how quickly he came up with the plan to get something as precious and valuable as the birthright. The birth order had sealed the ownership of the birthright.

Although they were twins, born only seconds apart, Esau was clearly the older and, therefore, the one to inherit the birthright. How unfair! But suddenly Jacob was presented with an opportunity to obtain the coveted birthright. Although the opportunity was unexpected, he was ready for it.

What Was the Birthright?

Once again, knowing the culture of the day makes this story so much more interesting. In Bible times, a man's inheritance, or the wealth he accumulated in his lifetime, was divided among his children upon his death. The eldest, however, got double the amount of the other brothers. He received what was known as the double portion of the inheritance.

If you were born a girl, then that's was just too bad. You got nothing, nada, zero, zip. After all, you were just a girl. Your role was to take care of the husband and his home, produce children for him, especially sons, and, of course, take care of those children.

If a man had four sons, his inheritance was divided into five portions. Each son got one fifth, but the eldest received two fifths. In Isaac's case, since he had two sons, his inheritance would eventually be divided into three portions, with Esau receiving two of those portions.

Selling Destiny for a Pot of Soup

That day, when Esau gave up his birthright, the double portion of his inheritance, he was giving up all the wealth Isaac had inherited from Abraham, who, to put it in modern terms, had the wealth of Bill Gates and Donald Trump put together. He was also giving up all the wealth Isaac himself had accumulated in his lifetime.

When people fail to recognize what's important to God, they'll go after what's important to them.

In addition to the thousands of cattle, sheep, oxen, and asses, (which were the money of the day), Abraham also had many servants. But included in the inheritance, which was really more important than all of the money, was the land of Canaan, the land which God Himself had given to Abraham. The land of Canaan was valuable, but Esau didn't recognize its value, so he gave up the land, the wealth, and his destiny—all for a pot of soup.

When people fail to recognize what's important to God, they'll go after what's important to them. God says, *"For my thoughts are not your thoughts, neither are your ways my ways"* (Isaiah 55:8). If we take the time to get to know God, He'll reveal what's valuable to Him. If not, we can then find ourselves going through life pursuing pots of soup.

This book is about pursuing purpose and overcoming the pain that comes with it. During times of pain, it will be essential to know that your purpose is important to God. If you don't, you'll be in danger of becoming an Esau and selling your purpose for a pot of soup.

The brief moments Esau took to think over Jacob's offer reminds me of an auctioneer in a room of prospective buyers. A bid is on the floor. Those in the audience are considering: am I willing to pay that price? The auctioneer intones, "Going once … going twice…" and then he pauses. When Esau failed to pay the price of waiting for food that didn't have such a high price tag and, instead, said, *"I swear,"* there was the sound of the spiritual gavel hitting the podium and the words "Gone! Sold to the highest bidder!" The birthright now belonged to Jacob, and that was the end of it.

When Deception Is Justified

Jacob had, in essence, stolen his brother's birthright. But it didn't stop there. Remember, we talked earlier about a man passing down his wealth to his eldest son upon his death. Well, before the man died, he passed down something else to this eldest son; it was called "the blessing." Now, "the blessing" had far-reaching implications. It was not only powerful, in that it made the eldest son the head of the tribe or clan. He was, in essence, the king over his family. But "the blessing" also carried with it just that—the future blessings and favor of God.

After Esau had sold his birthright to Jacob, he realized what he had done—even though it was already too late. Deep down, he resented Jacob, not necessarily because Jacob *got* the birthright from him (Esau didn't seem to be a long-range planner), but because of *how* Jacob got it. In any case, Esau knew, "the blessing" was still his. Little did he know that Jacob would eventually end up with this too. It happened in this way.

As Isaac grew older, he lost his sight. Soon now, he would be passing from the scene, and therefore he would need to pass on his blessing to his oldest son, Esau.

Although Esau had been entitled to the birthright, which would have given him a double portion of his father's inheritance, that was now gone. Now Rebekah, their mother, decided that Esau didn't deserve the blessing either. Jacob deserved it much more.

Rebekah was probably right, for it was apparent that Jacob was the more spiritual of the twin brothers. (Esau appears to have been spiritually shallow.) God had given Rebekah a sign at their birth that indicated that Jacob would be the prevalent one, and Esau would be under him. Still, what Rebekah did was wrong. Since God had spoken this, it was God's responsibility to bring it to pass, not Rebekah's

God didn't need Rebekah's help; He could bless Jacob in His own way. Two wrongs never make a right. You can never get to a right destination by taking a wrong road, and you can never willfully sin against God and expect Him to bless your actions. A good motive never justifies a wrong act.

Helping God ... Again

On the day that Isaac chose to pass on his blessing to his son, he called Esau to his tent. He told his eldest son to go to the field and hunt and bring back some venison. He really loved Esau's venison stew. The two of them would eat, and then Isaac would lay his hands upon Esau and give him his blessing.

Considering Isaac's increasing blindness, Rebekah hatched a plot to deceive him. She dressed Jacob in some of Esau's clothes she had in her house. Then she wrapped some animal skins around his arms so that he would seem to be hairy like his brother. Next, she prepared a stew of goat's meat that was nearly identical in taste to the stew Esau was accustomed to cooking for his father. (Rebekah must have been a fantabulous cook!) She then sent Jacob to take it to Isaac quickly, so that her favorite son could receive the blessing before Esau came back from his hunt.

When Jacob entered Isaac's tent, Isaac was very surprised that his son had accomplished so much in so little time. After all, Esau would have had to go to the field, hunt down a deer, kill it, clean it, cut it up, and then cook it. This process would have taken quite a long time. When Isaac inquired about how it was possible to do all of this so quickly, Jacob lied and said that God had blessed him to find the deer quickly. (Imagine, Jacob was lying on God!)

Isaac was somewhat suspicious, for it sounded to him like Jacob, not Esau. He told his son to come closer so that he could feel his hairy arms. He then kissed him. Smelling Esau's clothes, he finally put his suspicions at rest, and despite his misgivings, he proceeded to bless Jacob.

Right after Jacob received the sought-after blessing and had quickly left the scene of the theft, in came Esau. It was always a momentous occasion, when "the blessing" was passed down from the father to son, and Esau was overjoyed by the moment. He was in good spirits. *"Let my father arise, and eat of his son's venison, that thy soul may bless me,"* Esau ecstatically exclaimed (Genesis 27:31).

Something was wrong. In distress, Isaac was barely able to whisper, *"Who art thou?"* (Verse 32).

Esau, in bewilderment, answered, *"I am thy son, thy firstborn, Esau"* (Verse 32).

Isaac began to violently tremble. He asked who it was that had come in before Esau with stew. Who was it that he had blessed. Realizing the permanent nature of "the blessing," even under these circumstances, Isaac said, *"And he shall be blessed"* (Verse 33).

Grasping the magnitude of what had transpired, Esau was distraught. He was beside himself with pain. *"He cried with a great and exceeding bitter cry"* (Verse 34). Then he hysterically asked his father to bless him anyway, his pain evidenced in his words: *"Hast thou but one blessing, my father? bless me, even me also, O my father. And Esau lifted up his voice, and wept"* (Verse 38).

Isaac now realized that Jacob had deceived him, but the matter was out of his control. He told Esau that he had already given "the blessing" to Jacob, and, with that, he had made Jacob lord of the family.

Esau couldn't bear the thought of losing "the blessing." He had already sold his birthright. Now, both of his precious gifts, as the firstborn, were gone. He painfully asked his father if perhaps he didn't have one more blessing that he could give to him, and he *"lifted his voice, and wept."*

The Consequences of Our Choices

Pain is often quickly followed by anger. This event, left Esau so filled with hatred for Jacob that he vowed to kill him as soon as his father died. Jacob, fearing for his life, was forced to leave home quickly. His mother suggested that he go stay with her people in Padan-Aram for a while. Hopefully, by the time he got back home, Esau would have cooled down.

As in the case of Sarah helping God, when Rebekah decided that God needed help to fulfill His word to her, she had no idea of the consequences she would bear. It's always like that. Expect to suffer when you knowingly deceive someone, when you knowingly steal from someone.

Yes, Rebekah got what she wanted and had planned for. Jacob was now the recipient of both the birthright and the blessing. But that day Rebekah lost both of her sons. Esau now hated his mother, and Jacob was leaving. Little did Rebekah know at the time that, because of her choice to deceive, she would never again see her beloved Jacob.

What a big price to pay! Sin has a high cost. Rebekah got what she wanted, but look what she lost in the process.

Hearing the Voice of God

Isaac had many warnings to show him that something was amiss in the situation, but despite all of them, he chose to proceed with the blessing over his son. Just as He did with Isaac, God often tells us something over and over, but because we want to believe differently, we *choose* to believe differently. This often happens with people we meet and become enamored with. Our friends try to warn us about them, but we don't want to listen. Our parents try to warn us, but we refuse to heed their warning.

Then, suddenly, a movie is shown on television. It has a similar plot. Someone is not who or what they appear to be. We wonder if this might have any connection to the situation. Still, we don't listen.

The dog even barks when this person comes to visit. Even he senses that something is not right. We still don't listen. And because of our desire to believe what we want to believe, we then find ourselves in "messes" that affect us for years to come.

People and circumstances are very often not what they appear to be. So take your time. Pray. Ask God to give you a spirit of discernment. Ask Him to show you the answer to what you need to know, and then put aside your own desires and wait on God.

CHAPTER 3

---◆◇◆---

Your Past and Purpose

When Jacob left home, he went to the land of his mother in search of a suitable wife. What happened there is both very romantic and very tragic.

No sooner had Jacob arrived in the land than he saw a place where flocks of sheep were gathered at a well waiting to be watered, and he asked the shepherds gathered near the well if they knew his Uncle Laban. They said they did.

"Is he well?" Jacob asked.

"He is," he was told, and then the shepherds noticed a young lady coming through the fields leading some sheep. "That," they said, "is Laban's daughter coming now."

Love at First Sight

As the maiden came into view, Jacob stood mesmerized. Rachel was breathtakingly beautiful, and apparently it was love at first sight.

Jacob greeted Rachel and told her who he was, and then he quickly rolled the stone from the mouth of the well, so that her flocks could be watered. Next, he gave Rachel the customary greeting of a kiss and openly wept with joy, giving thanks to God. He had found the love of his life, just that quickly, and just that easily.

Jacob soon met Laban, his uncle, and he was welcomed to stay in Laban's house. At the first opportunity that presented itself, Jacob didn't waste any time in telling his uncle that he was in love with his daughter Rachel and wanted to marry her. That was fine, Laban said, but he would have to work for her for seven years.

At the very least, this must have given Jacob momentary pause. True, he had gotten himself into trouble with his father and his brother Esau, and it was probably a good idea for him to stay away from home for a while at least, but he was very close to his mother, and it would be hard for him to think of not seeing her again for seven long years.

Still, as the saying goes, "A son is a son until he finds a wife; a daughter is a daughter for the rest of her life." Jacob had found a wife, and he did not hesitate long in answering Laban. Working seven years for Rachel was no problem. If that's what it took, he was ready and willing to do it, because of his awesome love for her. And so, for the next seven years Jacob served his uncle.

A Time of Celebration Turns into A Time of Anger and Frustration

And Jacob served seven years for Rachel; and they seemed unto him but a few days, for the love he had to her.

Genesis 29:20

The seven years seemed to fly by, but at the end of that time, Jacob was more than ready to receive his bride in waiting. During those years, he had observed her from a proper distance, and he had come to love her more every day. It had gotten to the point that his love for Rachel was all consuming, and he must have been the brunt of many jokes because of it. But he couldn't help himself. He was in love, and his Rachel was all that he could think about. Now, at last, the time for their union had come, and he was delirious with joy.

Laban called for a weeklong celebration, and neighbors and relatives joined in the festivities to congratulate the bride and groom on their happy occasion. Then, at last, Jacob stood beside his bride (who was heavily veiled for the ceremony), the blessing was pronounced over the two of them, and in the gathering twilight, he retired to his tent to await her soon arrival.

We can only imagine the conversation between them during the moments that ensued. Jacob was elated, probably very nervous, and not a little bit intimidated.

Every nerve was tingling. He was a very happy man—to say the least. His dream had finally come true. He was now the husband of a very beautiful and desirous woman.

One can just imagine the scene. He must have called her name in those moments and said something like this: "Oh Rachel, Rachel, I love you so much. Can you believe it? The seven years are over. Rachel, I have dreamed over and over of this day. I thank my God for you, Rachel. Oh, Rachel, Rachel, Rachel!"

We can only imagine what might have been said on that wedding night, but what is not left to our imaginations is the fact that it was all a cruel hoax. The next morning, the deliriously happy Jacob opened his eyes, as the first rays of sun pierced the darkened sky, and found himself looking into the face, not of his beloved Rachel, but of her older sister Leah!

According to babynameworld.com, the name *Rachel* means "ewe" or "little lamb," and the name *Leah* means, "cow." Jacob expected to find his little lamb there by his side in the morning, and instead he found "cow." What a shock that must have been! According to the same source, another meaning of the name Leah is "weak-eyed." In that time, children were named for some characteristic, and Leah seems to have had something wrong with one or both of her eyes.

What was going on? Jacob must have lunged up in horror and unbelief. Where was his beautiful bride Rachel? What was unattractive Leah doing in bed with him? If this was someone's idea of a joke, he didn't find it to be funny in the least. He had paid a heavy price, seven years of manual labor, for the woman he loved, and now this? Somebody would pay for this. Where was Laban?

Jacob was furious, and he ran and found his father-in-law and complained to him in the strongest terms.

Laban had anticipated this, when, in the moments before the wedding, he had ordered Rachel to Leah's tent. He also ordered the two of them to exchange clothes, so that Leah, in Rachel's wedding garb, would be married to Jacob.

Jacob, it seems, had been so enthralled with the moment that he had never noticed that Rachel's own sister, Leah, was not present at the wedding. Now, he was understandably angry. Yes, Laban had been waiting for Jacob, and was ready with his answer.

It was against the custom of his people, he explained to his new son-in-law as calmly as possible, that a younger daughter should be given in marriage while an older sister remained unmarried. He was now married to Leah, and there was nothing he could do about it. Like it or not, that was the case.

When this revelation was made, and Laban had thus left Jacob with no recourse, I can imagine the young man standing there trembling with anger and frustration. How could this have happened to him? How could his mother's brother, his own flesh and blood, have so wrongfully deceived him? He didn't want Leah. He didn't want her at all. He had now made that point very obvious, but Laban had given him no way out. What could he do now?

What Goes Around Comes Around

What Jacob had to realize was that what goes around comes around. He had deceived his own father and brother, both of them his own flesh and blood, and now the tables had been turned on him. The deceiver had received a dose of his own medicine, as always happens, because the law of sowing and reaping is inviolable.

The remarkable thing about this event is how easily Laban was able to deceive Jacob. They had no electricity in those days, and Leah had entered Jacob's tent in the darkness of night. Because of that darkness, Laban's plan had worked perfectly.

I've heard it said on several occasions that God has a sense of humor, and this event makes me believe it. As I said before, what goes around comes around. Seven years earlier, Jacob had deceived his father, who, as a result of his blindness, lived in a state of darkness, now he got a taste of his own medicine, as he, too, was deceived in the dark.

When People Do You Wrong, God Pays the Debt

It's also noteworthy to mention that, through this event, God stood firmly on the side of Esau. The fact that he was immoral and Godless had nothing to do with it. Jacob had done him wrong, and God now punished Jacob for it.

Many hours are wasted by wronged people planning speeches that they will never get to deliver.

Isaac had done nothing to chastise Jacob for his wrongful deceit. If Jacob had not fled to Padan-Aram, Esau would have killed him. From this we see that it's never necessary to take revenge into our own hands. When people do you wrong, just remember what God says: *"Vengeance is mine, I will repay"* (Romans 12:19).

Many hours are wasted by wronged people planning speeches that they will never get to deliver. If they did deliver them, they know that they would "mess up" their testimony. People spend countless hours planning how *they* will get back at the person who has mistreated them. Let me encourage you. You can stop planning vengeance. God saw that person wrong you, and you don't need to taint your testimony or dirty your hands. God will pay your debt.

God can take vengeance for you much better that you can do it on yourself. Can you imagine that Esau could ever have planned a more wonderful and just punishment for Jacob? Of course not! And just as Esau had been so filled with hurt and anger over his stolen birthright, Jacob now felt the same hurt and anger over his stolen bride.

Also note that Esau was unaware that God had vindicated him. In the same way, there will be many times in life when God will vindicate you and you'll be unaware of it. That is between God and the offender. All you need to know is that God has a problem with those who wrong His children.

Now it all came back to Jacob. So this is what it felt like to be deceived! He didn't like it one bit, but there was nothing he could do about it. He was helpless.

Jacob, the trickster, had been tricked into marrying the wrong woman. He who had fooled his father had now been fooled himself. He had done his own wicked deed under the cover of darkness, and now, under the cover of darkness, he had been horribly wronged.

He was sorry now for what he had done, but it was too late. He had to pay the price, and it was a big one.

Seeing Jacob's obvious distress, and knowing his love for Rachel, the wheels of Laban's mind started rolling. Why not profit from this situation? With Jacob's great love for Rachel, he could probably get some more free years of labor out of him. So Laban made a suggestion. If Jacob was willing to work for him another seven years, he could marry Rachel too, and then he would have both of the sisters as wives.

What could Jacob do? He hadn't wanted Leah in the first place, but he now had no choice in the matter. They were married, and he had consummated the union on their wedding night. The idea of being able to have Rachel too definitely appealed to him, and somewhat appeased him, but he didn't like the idea of having to work another seven years for her. That suddenly seemed like a very long time to wait.

Well, Laban explained to Jacob, he wouldn't actually have to wait that long to marry Rachel. He could have her on credit, so to speak, and pay for her over time. If Jacob would just give Leah her week of honeymoon, Laban explained, he would arrange another wedding to follow it, and Jacob could, at last, be married to the woman he loved.

Jacob didn't seem to have any alternative. It was this or nothing, and he couldn't bear the thought of working so many years and coming up empty handed. He would marry Rachel, work another seven years to pay for her, and accept Leah as his booby prize. He didn't want her, and he didn't know what he would do with her, but he had no choice in the matter. And so he celebrated his second wedding a week after his first.

The Classic Struggle between Two Sisters

Jacob worked fourteen years because of his love for Rachel, and he got Leah thrown into the bargain. This set up a classic struggle between the two sisters. Anytime you have two women loving the same man, you have a fight on your hands, but this one was even more complicated.

Rachel was beautiful and greatly loved by Jacob, and Leah was unattractive and greatly resented. It must have been humiliating for Leah on her wedding night as she went through the ordeal of having sex with a man who was calling her sister's name in the process. Her long awaited wedding night had to have been a nightmare, as she listened to Jacob saying over and over how much he loved his Rachel.

With tears streaming down her face, Leah remained in utter silence through this whole ordeal. She couldn't afford to have her father's deception exposed. "Maybe it won't be so bad," she may have thought. "Maybe when he wakes up he'll be glad that it's me. I'm his wife now, not Rachel." Leah lay there in the dark listening to Jacob breathing. "God let him love me like he loves her," she must have prayed.

And then the next morning came, and with it, what must have been terrible beyond words for Leah, seeing the utter horror in Jacob's eyes. "Where's Rachel?" is all she heard. At that moment, looking into his eyes, she realized the awful truth: He didn't want her, and he didn't love her. In that moment, he actually loathed her, and the idea of having her as his wife repulsed him. All Jacob wanted was Rachel.

And that was just the beginning. What must their week of "honeymoon" have been like? Every time Jacob looked at Leah, he remembered the deception she had taken part in. He wanted his little ewe, his little lamb, but somehow he had been saddled with this unwanted weak-eyed woman. It was maddening. But if this arrangement was frustrating for Jacob and Rachel, it must have been even more so for poor Leah. Because of that, God took pity on her.

God Honored Leah

Jacob was faithful to pay lip service to Leah, but their relationship could not have been a mutually satisfying one. God saw, however, that Leah was hated and Rachel was loved, so He compensated Leah by allowing her to conceive first:

The Journey From Pain to Purpose

And when the Lord saw that Leah was hated, he opened her womb: but Rachel was barren.

Genesis 29:31

Being hated is sometimes a sure way to receive God's blessings, so don't despair when you're the one being hated. Instead, look for blessings to come your way. God is the defender of those who are hated.

For all of the Leahs who are reading this book (those whose husbands have walked out on you or taken another lover on the side, and those who are otherwise despised, disdained, hated, and rejected), there is good news. If your someone is not treating you right, God Himself will prepare a table before you in the presence of the one who despises you, and He will bless you openly. You just stay holy, be the best person you can be in God's sight, and watch God go into action on your behalf.

As for Leah, she had another problem—besides being unwanted by Jacob. In spite of his hatred for her, Leah truly loved Jacob, and she desperately wanted him to love her too.

When God saw that Leah was hated, He blessed her and opened her womb. She gave birth to a son, whom she named Reuben, meaning "behold, a son," for she said, *"Surely the LORD hath looked upon my affliction; now therefore my husband will love me"* (Genesis 29:32).

It was true that God had looked upon Leah's situation, but Leah had at least two very wrong concepts about her newborn son. (1) She was not as thrilled about having a son as she was about the hope of impressing Jacob and gaining his affections, and (2) She was sure that having this child would cause Jacob to love her. Sadly, many women have made and continue to make this same mistake. Having a child for a man does not earn his respect or love. Instead, far too many mothers are left alone to fend for themselves and their children because the man who sired them never really loved them.

What often happens is that when the woman becomes pregnant, the man abandons her and leaves her to give birth to the child and raise it on her own. She struggles, raising the child alone, while he eventually settles down with a woman he respects.

This is where many of our teenage girls err. They are convinced that having sex with their boyfriend will cause him to love them, but it hasn't, and it won't.

Why Buy the Cow, When You Can Get the Milk for Free?

When a woman succumbs to a man's advances and has sex outside of marriage, it often does just the opposite. As soon as the man has conquered his new challenge, there comes a loss of respect, and off he goes in search of another conquest. I know many women who would actually be married today had they not fallen into this trap. After all, why buy the cow, when you can get the milk for free? Men love a challenge, not an easy woman.

Your praise to God is not based on what He does for you, but on who He is.

Many Christians have seen this happen to daughters and granddaughters, and it's always a tragedy. Some men seem to sense desperation in others and know how to take advantage of it.

Leah was slow to learn her lesson. She tried again and again to gain Jacob's love through having more of his children. Soon after Reuben's birth, Leah gave birth to a second son whom she named Simeon, meaning "hearing with acceptance," for she said, *"Because the LORD hath heard that I was hated"* (Genesis 29:33). When the next son came along, she named him Levi, meaning "adhesion" or "joined." She said, *"This time will my husband be joined unto me"* (Genesis 29:34).

It may have been that when Leah's fourth son was born, she was beginning to learn a lesson. She called this child Judah, meaning "praise." She said, *"Now will I praise the Lord"* (Genesis 29:35).

Praising God in the Midst of our Trials

I suppose you could say that Leah was praising the Lord because she thought she was ahead in the war to win Jacob's heart, but I would like to think that, this time, she had decided to praise the Lord in spite of how Jacob felt about her. This is what true praise is all about.

Your praise to God is not based on what He does for you, but on who He is. Sometimes, as in Leah's situation, we give the sacrifice of praise, (similar to the act of giving a sacrificial offering). When you give something you have little of, it's called a sacrifice. There are times in life when we don't understand why we're going through some situation or circumstance. During these times, you may not think you have a lot of praise to give to God. In the midst of these painful times, you even wonder, "Where is God? Does He see my tears? Does He hear my prayers?" Because the heavens are silent, we decide to hold back on our praise.

Let me give you a word of encouragement: Even though the heavens are silent, God is still on the throne! He sees your situation. He sees your pain. If he has not moved on your behalf, it simply isn't time. You will not always be in this situation. When it's time, I promise that God will move on your behalf. Until then, be like Leah and determine, "Now, I will praise God."

As for Jacob, he would go to his grave loving Rachel more than he loved Leah, and nothing Leah could do would ever change that fact. All of her desperate finagling got her absolutely nowhere.

The Charged Atmosphere

The fact that Leah had given birth to four sons in short order was a terrible affront to Rachel, who was still unable to conceive. In the charged atmosphere of the day, this was scandalous. A woman who brought no children into the world was not considered to be a real woman. She was not fulfilling the purpose she was born for. In later years, barrenness would be registered as acceptable grounds for divorce.

The sense of reproach in Rachel's case was even more real because all of Leah's children were sons. Girls may have been appreciated in those days, but boys were treasured. The wife who gave life to sons was highly regarded by the family and the community, and this caused her man to be greatly admired and envied. Even if Jacob didn't love Leah, he most likely appreciated her and was proud to have her four sons. This gave Leah another definite advantage.

To my way of thinking, one of the greatest tragedies to come out of all of this strife was that Rachel allowed her jealousy for her sister to affect her relationship with Jacob, and they argued over it:

And when Rachel saw that she bare Jacob no children, Rachel envied her sister; and said unto Jacob, Give me children, or else I die. And Jacob's anger was kindled against Rachel: and he said, Am I in God's stead, who hath withheld from thee the fruit of the womb?

Genesis 30:1-2

This is another great lesson women everywhere can learn from this story. Jacob and Rachel loved each other, but they allowed the issue of Leah's children to cause conflict in their marriage.

When you see another woman making eyes at your husband (and it happens in the church, as well as in the world), don't attack your husband as if he has done something wrong. Most women say nothing to the other woman (which, in most cases, they should not), but then they proceed to accuse their husbands:

"What did you say to her?"

"What did she say to you?"

"I saw the way you looked at her."

"Why do you have to be so friendly with her?"

"Don't you think I know what's going on?"

"You're just jealous," the husband usually responds. But a year down the road, when the woman has become more brazen in her approach, he may realize that you were right all along. The way you handle the situation will make all the difference in your continued relationship with your husband.

If a husband fails to recognize it when some other woman is trying to win his favor, that's his problem, not his wife's. Wives cannot live their husband's life for him. You are not his Holy Spirit, and you can't always be following him around, making sure he doesn't do something wrong. If a man or woman is bent on doing wrong, you can stop them for only so long. If God can't control them, what makes you think that you can?

If you're a wife, all you can do is pray, treat him right, cook for him (even if you would rather shoot him), and, by all means, take care of him in the bed. If your man is being tempted, you don't want the enemy using you to give him an excuse to do wrong.

Finally, don't make the classic mistake I see so many young wives making, that of fussing and "cussing." When you do this, not only will he leave; you have just helped him justify his leaving.

If you're willing to do these things and do them as unto the Lord, being the best wife you can possibly be, you can help your husband not look the other way. If he still chooses to do wrong, he will most assuredly feel some guilt over his sin, and find no justification for it.

As a wife, find out what your man likes, and try to keep yourself attractive for him. When you have done all that, and he still doesn't recognize what he has in you, all you can do is pray and leave the matter in God's hands.

Wrestling with My Sister

The pressure to produce children, especially male children, was so strong upon Rachel that she eventually decided to take very rash measures. She felt that she had no choice but to give Jacob her personal servant Bilhah as a concubine, so that he could have children by her. As we have seen from the case of Abraham and Sarah, this was a fairly common practice of the day. That, however, didn't make it any easier for Rachel to do.

Bilhah produced two sons for Jacob, and since these sons were considered by most people to be Rachel's own, she was afforded the privilege of naming them. The first she called Dan, meaning "judge," for she said, *"God hath judged me, and hath also heard my voice, and hath given me a son"* (Genesis 30:6). The second son was named Naphtali, which meant "my wrestling" or "my twisting," for she said, *"With great wrestlings have I wrestled with my sister, and I have prevailed"* (Genesis 30:8).

What a sad situation! Sisters should love each other and be friends. But when two sisters are in love with the same man, sisterly love falls by the wayside. These two sisters were living side-by-side and constantly vying for their man's affections. That would be a recipe for explosive behavior in any society. This was a household filled with conflict, competition, jealousy, and strife, and it would only get worse with time.

These two women were in a never-ending contest for their man's love, and this was not surprising. If there is one thing women cannot share, it's their man.

They can share almost anything else. They can share favorite recipes, even giving away a secret family ingredient. They can share the responsibility of caring for their children, and they're even willing to share their clothes at times. But don't ask them to share the love of the same man. Rachel and Leah may have been sisters, but they had now become bitter opponents on a very real battlefield.

Sisters should love each other and be able to talk openly and honestly with each other, but these two sisters didn't and couldn't. Instead, they wrestled with each other over every minute detail of life. And, worst of all, their poor children were caught in the middle of this endless tug of war.

Another Concubine Added to the Mix

When Leah saw what Rachel had done, she gave her own personal servant Zilpah to Jacob to bear him more children, and he fathered two more sons by this concubine. One of Zilpah's sons was named Gad, meaning "good fortune," because Leah said, *"A troop cometh"* (Genesis 30:11). The other son was named Asher, meaning "happy" or "fortunate," because Leah said, *"Happy am I, for the daughters will call me blessed"* (Genesis 30:13). But the coming of these additional sons did nothing to reduce the tensions in the household. They only seemed to increase with each new turn of events.

Let's see, what was the score now? By now, eight children had been born in this family. Leah had four sons. Bilhah, Rachel's maid had birthed two sons. Zilpah, Leah's maid, had birthed two sons. The score was now 6 to 2 in Leah's favor.

The Strange Story of the Mandrakes

And then we have the very strange story of the mandrakes. Here is what the Bible says:

And Reuben went in the days of the wheat harvest, and found mandrakes in the field, and brought them unto his mother Leah. Then Rachel said to Leah, Give me, I pray thee, of thy son's mandrakes.

And she [Leah] said unto her, Is it a small matter that thou hast taken my husband? and wouldest thou take away my son's mandrakes also?

And Rachel said, Therefore he shall lie with thee tonight for thy son's mandrakes.

And Jacob came out of the field in the evening, and Leah went out to meet him, and said, Thou must come in unto me; for surely I have hired thee with my son's mandrakes. And he lay with her that night.

Genesis 30:14-16

It appears, that although he had two wives and two concubines to please, Jacob spent most of his time with Rachel. The mandrakes Reuben found in the field were thought to have the power to induce fertility. Rachel therefore wanted them, thinking that they might help her to conceive. Mandrakes were also highly prized as an aphrodisiac. Leah therefore wanted them, too, thinking that they might help her to win Jacob's love.

Leah initially criticized Rachel for the audacity of her request. It seems that, in the midst of battle, she had experienced convenient amnesia. She lashed out at Rachel for taking her husband, forgetting that it was Rachel who had been Jacob's intended bride. Plus, it wasn't Rachel's fault that Jacob did not love Leah.

Still, because Leah was continually looking for ways to win Jacob's heart, she was not averse to using this desire on Rachel's part as a means of luring Jacob away from her—if only for a single night of passion. The mandrakes appeared to be a perfect tradeoff.

Thus, Leah hired Jacob from Rachel for the night, and Rachel agreed to this exchange. Rachel was desperate for a child. If she had to give up Jacob for a night, it was worth it.

There was a surprising twist in Rachel's plan. Although Rachel was now in possession of some of the much-desired mandrakes, Leah was the one who became pregnant. She gave birth to a fifth son named Issachar. Shortly after that, to add further grief to Rachel, Leah had her sixth and final son.

As for Leah, she was still fighting to win Jacob's love. When this son was born, she said, *"Now will my husband dwell with me,"* and so she named him Zebulon, meaning "dwelling" (Genesis 30:20).

Poor Leah! All of this was still done in an effort to win Jacob's heart. She may have been Jacob's first wife, but she was definitely "the other woman," and she struggled constantly to gain a better footing in his heart.

Eventually, she bore Jacob a daughter, whom she named Dinah. But in all of the confusion, poor Dinah may have not gotten much attention at all.

This is such an interesting situation. Here Leah was with six sons, but she would have done anything to have the love of Jacob. On the other hand, here was Rachel with the undying love of Jacob, but she would have done anything to have a son. As they say, the grass is always greener on the other side of the fence.

What both women failed to realize is some things are beyond our control. On Leah's part, as we have previously discussed, a woman cannot control a man's heart by having his children. Although he may be grateful (in some cases, at least), gratefulness and love are two entirely different emotions.

On Rachel's part, she failed to understand that it is God who opens and closes wombs. Rachel was using her own efforts—giving Jacob her maid Bilhah, buying Reuben's mandrakes, and, as we will see later, relying on her father's idols—to obtain a child. This may have been why God delayed her pregnancy.

What a lesson we can all learn from this! Too often, people look to their own strength and to other people to do what only God can do. Because of this, God often allows us to get to the place that no one can help us, and we cannot help ourselves, before He chooses to move on our behalf. This is the reason, that whenever we are going through some trial, we need to recognize that God has His own agenda.

God is not interested in being a spiritual Santa Claus. During our times of need, He wants us to turn to Him. His first agenda is to take us from faith to faith, from one level of faith in Him to an ever higher level.

The Dysfunctional Family

I think Rachel finally got it. She finally cried out to God to open her womb, and in the end, He heard that cry. She bore a son, and she named him Joseph, meaning "added," because she was sure that God would add yet more children to her. She was right. A few years later, she would bear one more son, Benjamin. But she was to die tragically giving birth to him.

Joseph, then, was born into what we have come to call in modern society "a blended family." Such families are nothing new. It is only the proliferation of blended families that is relatively new to American society.

Joseph was thus born into a household that was far from normal. He was born into the midst of a wrestling match, a struggle for respect and love. He was a member of a seriously dysfunctional family.

What an interesting household! This was the complicated atmosphere in which little Joseph grew up.

When Rachel died, Joseph was suddenly left alone in this diverse group with their competing interests. Living with such conflicted people must have been a challenge for him, and yet from an early age, he seems to have stood out from the crowd.

CHAPTER 4

—➤•◄—

The Legacy of Jealousy

And it came to pass, when Joseph was come unto his brethren, that they stript Joseph out of his coat, his coat of many colours that was on him.

Genesis 37:23

The Atmosphere of Hatred

Since early childhood, Jacob's older sons grew up resenting their Aunt Rachel. They had watched their mother desperately trying to win their father's affections. They had seen her moments of pain over the situation. And, right or wrong, they saw Rachel as the reason they and their mother had to play second fiddle. Because they hated Rachel, they also hated Joseph.

They had now lived with constant strife for so long that it had become a part of who they were. Through the years, as they watched their mother and their Aunt Rachel constantly wrestling for favor, it left a deposit in their lives. Now they had a permanent legacy from their mothers.

But this was not the kind of legacy mothers dream of leaving their sons. This was something ugly and nasty, a *legacy of jealousy* and hatred, and it had passed from mother to sons and was now negatively affecting their everyday lives.

I have watched this happen many times. Children have no problem with a certain individual … until their mother or father has a problem with that person. The children then begin supporting this attitude, and a dramatic change comes over them. This should not surprise us. Attitudes are catching, and children catch them very easily.

My husband tells the story of a teacher giving a lecture on how receptive children are in their formative years. She wanted the audience to know the importance of teaching children during this time. "Children are like sponges," she said. "They soak up everything you pour into them." One man commented, "You're right, but children are like sponges in more ways than that. They also soak up everything you spill."

Children are very perceptive, and they easily take on the attitudes of their parents and repeat words they have heard them say. This is especially true of their mothers, since they spend so much time with them in their early years. Both parents, however, should be aware that they're being watched and imitated.

Also, children everywhere want to be loyal to their mothers (especially girls), and if Mama doesn't like someone, then they can't like that person either. Because of this, I have always tried to be careful never to discuss any personal differences I had with other people in front of my four sons. If my children wanted to befriend a person who had done me wrong in the past, although it was difficult, I tried to accept this. God holds us accountable for any legacy of bitterness that we pass on to our children.

Boys are always protective to their mothers, and when these boys saw their mother being neglected and overlooked, it hurt them deeply. It was not logical for them to hate Rachel and her son for that, but that's just human nature.

If the two mothers had found it in their hearts to forgive each other, this bitterness might not have been passed on to their children. But they didn't, so this legacy of jealousy was passed on down to the next generation through the mothers.

The Fateful Coat

Jacob then did something that was probably unwise and that apparently caused even more family strife. He gave Joseph a special coat, a coat the Bible describes simply as *"a coat of many colors."* What was this coat? And why did it cause so much contention?

Everything about the coat was significant. The common coats of the day were knee length and short sleeved or sleeveless, as this gave the wearer more freedom to work. Joseph's coat, in contrast, was long sleeved and fell to the ankle, indicating that he was a person of privilege, not having to work as the others did.

Secondly, the coat was ornately decorated, much like the garments of princes or nobles of the day. In this way, Jacob was signifying the role he expected his son Joseph to play in the future.

As Rebekah, his mother, had done for him, favoring him over his older brother, Esau, Jacob was now openly favoring the younger Joseph over his older brothers. As we will soon see, this caused many problems in the family.

Why would Jacob risk this? Didn't he have enough problems already? He had spent years trying to keep the peace among his mottled group of women and their children? Why complicate things even more?

The only explanation offered by the Bible is this: *"because he was the son of his old age"* (Genesis 37:3). That makes sense. But we also know that Joseph was the son of Jacob's beloved Rachel, and since Rachel was now only a memory, Joseph was something tangible from her that Jacob could cling to.

And yet there was more to the situation than even that. When Jacob gave his son a coat fit for royalty, he was performing a prophetic act. This son would rule. Jacob was sure of it.

The Tattletale

Jacob's gift to Joseph had to be a great disappointment to the other boys, and it made an already bad situation worse. Joseph had already exhibited typical youngest-child traits, which always get on the nerves of the older siblings.

Joseph, being seventeen years old, was feeding the flock with his brethren; and the lad was with the sons of Bilhah, and with the sons of Zilpah, his father's wives: and Joseph brought unto his father their evil report.

Genesis 37:2

45

In most families, the youngest child is treated differently from the others. By the time that youngest child comes along, the parents are often tired of disciplining their children, and have mellowed a lot in other ways as well. Consequently, the youngest child gets away with a lot the others could not have gotten away with. "If I had done that while I was growing up, you would have half killed me," the older children complain. And they may have a point.

In addition, younger children seem more demanding and self-absorbed. I believe this somewhat described Joseph. There can be no doubt that he was a very spoiled child.

As if all of this was not enough, one day Joseph returned from the fields to report to his father that his brothers were misbehaving, that their work was somehow inferior. This had to rub his brothers the wrong way.

Four of these boys were the sons of Jacob's concubines, Leah and Rachel's servant girls. As concubine's sons, they worked, and they worked hard. But Daddy's Baby Joseph did very little. Now *he* was going to report to his father that *their* work was substandard? They might be the sons of concubines, but Joseph was not their master, and Jacob was their father too. As far as they were concerned, Joseph was nothing but a spoiled brat and a tattletale, and he spelled trouble for their future.

To children, nothing is worse than a tattletale, and younger children are often guilty of it: "Mama, you told Jada to wash the dishes, and she didn't do it right. She put the pots away while they were still wet, and she didn't mop the floor like you told her to."

How very mature that little one seems at the moment. They delight in reporting on an older brother or sister. "Mama, while you were gone, Gloria's boyfriend came over. He stayed until just before you got home. He just left." (I remember telling this one to my mother about my oldest sister.)

Spoiled brothers and sisters often get their older siblings in trouble, and they're not well remembered for it either. Spoiled brats seem to get away with everything.

But there's more to it than that. By the time parents have their last child, they have more disposable income. When the older siblings were growing up, the parents barely made ends meet. Because things were tight, the older children were called upon to make many sacrifices, but by the time the *last* child comes along, the family is more financially established, and so the parents lavish things on that little one.

The older daughters may have received one dress from K-Mart, but now the younger children have a whole wardrobe from Nordstrom's. When an older child graduated from high school, they were just happy to get a diploma. Some may have gotten a gift of ten or, at the very most, twenty dollars. But when those babies come along, they often get a car for graduation.

As children grow to be adults and have their own families, they come to understand their parents' actions a little more. The special treatment the younger sibling received is now something they tease them about during family reunions. Just as parents tell their children that they don't know how good they have it (after all, *they* walked twenty miles uphill in the snow to get to school), now older siblings take the opportunity to let their younger siblings know just how spoiled they were. This is no longer an irritant. Instead, it's a family joke.

I know something about younger siblings. Gloria and I, as the oldest in our family, always had chores to do around the house. Little sister Dianna, who now directs our church choir, wasn't required to do any work at all. But we didn't hate her for that. That's just the way it is with younger siblings.

It is very possible that before Joseph came along, Jacob had shown more love to his other boys. They were, after all, his first children, so that would have been only natural. When Joseph came along, however, the rest of them seemed forgotten. Now it was just Joseph, Joseph, Joseph.

Jacob's Blatant Favoritism

And when his brethren saw that their father loved him more than all his brethren, they hated him, and could not speak peaceably unto him.

Genesis 37:4

It is probably not unusual for children to feel that a parent is showing favoritism to one of their siblings. They may or may not be right. In Jacob's case, it seems that the other children had every reason to complain. It was a mistake for Jacob to do this so blatantly. That had to be very hurtful to the other brothers.

Jacob should have known better. He had suffered long because his mother had shown favoritism to him over Esau, and this should have taught him how harmful developing such an attitude could be. I have four sons: Chuck, Chris, Corey and Cary. I love them all four and would never show any outright favoritism for one of them above the others.

On the other hands, I do understand why it sometimes happens. Often a family will have one child among several who is extremely cooperative and helpful to their parents, and it's hard for the parents, at times, not to show favoritism toward that child. He or she will seemingly do anything for their parents. When the parents ask the other children to take out the trash or wash the dishes, they act as if such a request is tantamount to child abuse.

These days, many children seem to become offended at the least little suggestion by their parents that they do anything. For instance, if they're told to move back from the television so that they won't ruin their eyesight, they "get an attitude." So it's only natural that parents would tend to dote on a child who has a more cooperative spirit and seems to be more loving and caring.

This may be what happened in the case of Joseph. Jacob saw something in the child that caused him to extend special favor to him. But that only worsened an already difficult home situation. Joseph's brothers came to hate him because of the favoritism displayed toward him by his father.

When a child, who has longed to be accepted and appreciated by his parents does not receive that acceptance, it leaves a deep-seated sense of loss. Every child wants to hear "well done," and to know that his parents are proud of him. Every child presents with pride their report card to Mom and Dad, hoping for their approval. Children look into the audience for their parents with expectation when participating in some program. They still do this on the football field and basketball court in older years. These boys were no different. They, too, wanted their father's attention. But as they grew older, it became increasingly apparent that Dad had a deeper love for Joseph than he did for the rest of them.

Still, the fact that Joseph's brothers hated him because of how their mothers were treated does not sufficiently explain the intensity of their hatred. Nor does the fact that Joseph was a tattletale or that Jacob failed to pay sufficient attention to his older sons. Something else contributed to their eventual rage, something that we must take time to explore further.

The Importance of a Father's Love

Joseph's brothers had been hurt many times as they grew up, and that hurt had left some permanent scars on their lives.

Joseph didn't help the situation. He was very self-absorbed, and his father fed this self-absorption by doting on him. This hurt the other brothers over and over again. Every living person needs to be appreciated and loved. Every child longs for his father to be proud of him. Jacob seems to have had difficulty identifying with his other sons as he did with Joseph. He was proud of Joseph, but he didn't appear to be proud of the rest of "the bunch." This hurt, and it hurt a lot.

An entire generation now needs psychological help because far too many children have grown up without the attention and love of a father.

This speaks to a major problem we are facing today in America. An entire generation now needs psychological help because far too many children have grown up without the attention and love of a father. This leaves something vitally missing from their lives. Because of so many broken families, we now see an increasing rise in gang activity. Interestingly, statistics show that a high percentage of gang members come from single parent homes and poorly blended families.

Young men need the example and discipline a father provides in the home. I often tell mothers that there's power simply in the presence of a man in the home.

Have you ever wondered why moms have to tell their children to do things several times before they finally move? She tells the child again and again what to do, each time raising her voice to a new level. They instinctively seem to recognize the pitch of danger in her voice, (usually about the third time she has

49

told them what she's going to do if they don't get up and move), and it's only then that they obey. Dads, on the other hand, usually only need to give the command once, and the children do as they are told.

As sons grow older, they often become bigger and stronger than their mothers. There comes a time when Mom can no longer spank her child as she has previously done. If that mother has not succeeded in putting some fear of her into her children while they were young, she will be in trouble when they get older. This is why many teenagers ignore their mother and do what they want. After all, what can she do about it?

Mothers in this situation do what they can. They fuss and threaten, but often that is the extent of their power. A man, on the other, hand can go strength to strength with unruly sons (and daughters), and children know the difference.

As previously mentioned, I have four sons. While they were young, although I showered them with love, I also taught them to fear me. A small dose of fear is healthy and necessary when raising children. That is ... unless you want your children to run your house.

There's nothing wrong with fear. We know that God loves us more than words can express, but sometimes it is our fear of Him that keeps us from doing all sorts of crazy things.

When one of my sons was about ten, he had the audacity to raise his hand to me. I believe the Bible's instruction on discipline:

He who spares his rod hates his son, but he who loves him disciplines him properly.

Proverbs 13:24 NKJ

Needless to say, because I loved my son, that was the last time he ever tried that. As a consequence, by the time my sons had become teenagers, on the rare occasion that they attempted to even voice some word of rebellion, I was able to put them in check with a few simple words: "You're not too big for me to spank." It didn't matter that I was only five-foot-one and weighed only a hundred and thirteen pounds. It worked for two reasons: (1) Their early childhood training had taught them to respect authority and fear discipline, and (2) If needed, their father was always there to back me up. It's a good thing to have a father in the home, and that's one reason that God gave children two parents.

Often teen pregnancy can also be traced back to this absence of the father in the home. Many times, young girls are looking for the love of a man in their lives, and because the man God ordained to love them first is missing, they fall for the wrong male too early. Besides providing his daughters with the love they need growing up, a father in the home provides them protection. A father also recognizes when a young man has wrong intentions toward his daughter. After all, he was once a teenager himself. Lastly, a father provides to his daughter an example of what a man should be. It is not unusual for a girl to marry a man with the same traits as her father.

Joseph's brothers wanted the love of their father, and they wanted Jacob to display the same love for them that he did to Joseph. They desperately desired his attention.

These brothers were angry because Joseph was getting what they wanted. Right or wrong, he seemed to be the source of their pain. Thus, they focused all of their frustration onto Joseph, and he became the object of their wrath.

Hurt Not Properly Dealt With

Life often brings with it times of deep disappointment. If the disappointment comes from people who are not close to us, we can often lay it aside. But, when the source of our disappointment comes from a loved one, this is not so easy. Yet, after the initial sting of the disappointment, no matter how difficult, we can often move on by telling ourselves, "They didn't mean it," or "They didn't realize what they were saying or doing."

But we can only justify disappointment so many times. At some point, we eventually come to realize that they did mean it, and they did know exactly what they were saying or doing. When we get to this point, we have to make a conscious decision either to let it go anyway or hold onto the wrongdoing.

When disappointment is not properly dealt with, it will eventually turn to hurt. At this point, we begin to wonder: "How could they do this? How could they say such things?" Once again, because the person is so close to us, this hurt wounds us. If we cannot somehow get past this, if this hurt is not properly dealt with, it will turn to anger.

"How could they do this to me? How could they say this to me?" We ask ourselves this question over and over. We simply can't understand it. After all, we wouldn't treat them this way.

We begin to spend hours planning speeches in our heads about what we're going to tell them. Most of it never gets said (and that's probably a very good thing).

The anger begins to fester. And, when anger is not properly dealt with, it turns to resentment.

If you take the time to study people, you can usually see when they're in this stage. Their resentment is usually evidenced in what is not said.

Let's say, for example, that you have a group of women at an outing, and one of them is going through a bitter season with her husband. He becomes the subject of conversation. The other women may say some nice things about him as a person or about something he has accomplished, but, although the wife does not negate this, she brings up something he has neglected to do. She cannot publicly appear to be angry, and she deeply resents the fact that she cannot just shout out what a horrible husband he is. He may be her hero again in six months, but presently he's the enemy. She is, in no way, about to join in the accolades for her husband. She wants to shine a negative light on him because she's in the stage of resentment.

If you take the time to watch and listen, resentment will show its ugly face. Often it will be seen more in what people are not saying or doing rather than in what they are. A lack of support for some program of yours or a failure to warn you of imminent danger could be a sign that resentment is growing against you. And if such resentment is not properly dealt with, it will turn to bitterness, the most dangerous of these stages.

If you have never been bitter, let me warn you: You don't want to go there. If, as you are reading this, you realize you are bitter and now see how you got there, take a word of advice and get out of there as fast as you possibly can.

Bitterness is probably the most dangerous of these stages. It's like a cancer; it eats you from the inside out. If left unchecked, it will eventually destroy you.

Bitterness is a dark, lonely abyss from which everything is now measured. *All* men are now dogs. Their whole family is "messed up." The relationship was *never* satisfying. They were *always* this way.

Such bitterness sets in when (1) People wrong you, (2) They get away with it, and (3) God doesn't intervene. Take the case of the office worker who has always been the first one on the job and the last one to go home at night. They have done this for years, and yet, over and over, they have been passed up for promotion. Now they're actually training someone with less knowledge, experience, and seniority to be their own boss.

Or take the case of the faithful wife who has tried to be everything for her husband, and he has now left her and his children and traded her in for a younger model. He now lives with another woman and takes care of her children, but, at the same time, won't give the money needed to care for his own.

Or take the talented athlete who was overlooked in his high school athletic program because of the color of his skin. The same thing happened to him when he entered the armed forces, and now he can't even find a job. Caught up in such situations, some people can become embittered from life.

In each of these cases, where is God? Why doesn't He intervene and zap the person, or, at the very least, expose them for what they truly are. If you were God, you would. "She's not the great wife people think she is." "He's not Mr. Wonderful."

We must remember that God has given us free will. He doesn't force us to do right. When men do you wrong, as we saw in Chapter Two, He repays them in full. You may never see it, but God is faithful, and He will vindicate you.

Bitterness Destroys Your Health

The problem with bitterness is that it destroys you, not them. It "messes" up your health, not theirs. While you're continually dwelling on how they wronged you, they've gone on with their life. While you're angrily glaring at them out the corner of your eye, they often don't even know you exist.

I've often said that bitterness steals your joy, then your song, then your health, and then your looks. Go to your twenty-year class reunion, and there take a look at the classmates who appear as if they could have been one of your teachers. Those are most likely the people whom bitterness has attacked.

If you happen to be in this sad state, let me take a moment to encourage you: You need to let it go and move on. You're going to end up with some disease if you don't. Our bodies were not meant to deal with long periods of bitterness and the stress that accompanies it.

When I come in contact with someone who has arthritis or some other disease that is affecting or afflicting their bones, I usually ask them if they're harboring some unforgiveness in their hearts. I ask this question because the Bible says that bitterness actually *"rots [our] bones"*:

A heart at peace gives life to the body, but envy rots the bones.

Proverbs 14:30, NIV

Obviously, all debilitating diseases are not due to unforgiveness, but when you lack peace in your heart, it can be detrimental to your health.

You Cannot Go Back and Relive the Past

At some point, you have to accept that it happened, it's over, and there's nothing you can do about it. You can't go back and relive the past. Let it go. I encourage you to pray. Ask God to give you the strength to forget, forgive, and move on with your life. It's time to put the past in the past.

The last stage in the cycle of bitterness is revenge. When bitterness is not dealt with, it eventually turns to revenge, which is the most destructive part of the cycle. Revenge simply says, "I'm going to get them!" and it either plans or simply waits for the proper moment to come.

Joseph's brothers went through all these stages during the years prior to their murderous attack on their little brother. Even though they ended up in the revenge stage, their hate began with hurt.

All of us experience bitterness to some degree. When we feel helpless and hopeless, we can become bitter against someone or some thing that is causing our discomfort. In the case of Joseph's brothers, they probably became angry and bitter at the wrong person. Joseph was still very young, and his frustrated and angry brothers probably should have directed their anger at Jacob instead. He was the one showing favoritism. He was the one who spoiled Joseph so terribly.

Showing favoritism to one child over another is always a problem, but in the highly charged atmosphere of a blended family, such as the one into which Joseph was born, it can be deadly. It is very common for a parent to want to do special things for their own child, and this leads to hurt feelings for those who are "her" child or "his" child. Sometimes a stepparent will go to the other extreme. In trying to be sure that they treat the stepchild no differently from their own natural child, they end up overcompensating. This brings complaints from their own children.

"You're my Mom (or Dad), and you're taking her side? I didn't want you to get married to 'him' in the first place, and now I'm the one who has to suffer. I don't like 'him,' and I don't like 'them.' " Living in a blended family can present a whole new realm of problems. One of the most important ways to begin defusing the atmosphere is to assure that children and stepchildren are treated equally. But that's never an easy task.

It is very possible that Jacob justified his special treatment of Joseph on the grounds that the child had lost his mother, but that didn't make it any easier for the other brothers to stomach. This special treatment was wrong, and in spite of any possible justification, it left them with a deep-seated resentment.

The School of Hard Knocks

One particular incident in Jacob's life seems to illustrate well this problem of favoritism that was now building to a dangerous climax: After living for twenty years in Padan-aram, the home of his Uncle Laban and his two wives, Jacob decided that it was time to take his family and return to Canaan.

Jacob had suffered greatly under Laban, almost deservedly. He had had to flee from his home because of his deception of Esau. This deception had left his brother so bitter that he planned to murder him. But we reap what we sow, and Jacob reaped just that. Even as Rebekah seemed to have had no problem helping deceive her son Esau, her brother Laban also seemed to have no problem deceiving his sister's child, his own nephew.

Remember, Jacob had worked for Laban for fourteen years for Rachel and Leah, seven of these years as a result of Laban's initial deceit concerning which of the girls Jacob would marry. When the fourteen years were completed, Laban convinced Jacob to continue working for him for pay, but in the ensuing years, Laban continued to deceive Jacob by using one excuse after another to change his agreed-upon wages.

Finally, Jacob completed his time in the school of hard knocks and God told him it was time to go home to Canaan.

Preparing to Meet Esau

There comes a time in life when we must go back and confront our past, no matter how difficult that might be. If God is to use you, He wants to wipe your slate clean so that your past doesn't come back to haunt you. This may involve righting wrongs you've done to others in the past—even though it is so much easier to forget about the wronged party and even to justify our actions. Such was the case with Jacob when God eventually directed him to return to Canaan.

What worried Jacob now was how Esau would receive him. Had he forgiven the theft of the birthright and the blessing? Or was Jacob's life still in serious danger? Would Esau harm his family as a means of taking revenge? He separated a portion of his herds as a gift to Esau to try to placate his anger, but would that be enough?

Jacob was determined to make things right with Esau, but he couldn't take for granted the fact Esau would be willing to reconcile with him. Esau just might try to do Jacob or his family harm.

On the morning of Jacob's meeting with Esau, he looked up and saw his brother swiftly approaching with four hundred men. Jacob became fearful for his family. Rather than risk the entire family, he decided to split them into groups.

In the first group, the one most likely to be attacked by Esau, he placed the two concubines and their four children. They were, therefore, in the most vulnerable position. Leah and her children followed them. Wanting to keep his favorites, Rachel and Joseph, farthest from harm, he placed them in the very rear, in the least likely spot to be attacked. What must Joseph's brothers have thought of that arrangement?

When Jacob placed these older sons in front of Joseph, what they heard Jacob saying was something like this: "You're on the bottom layer of my heart." I'd rather see you die before harm comes to my beloved Joseph. Can you imagine how that felt to a child? "Daddy wants to save Joseph at all costs, but he doesn't care about me. He would probably be happy if Mommy and me died. That would rid him of his problems." Such thoughts, once entertained, rarely leave a child. They just build and build to their inevitable climax.

————◆◇◆————

CHAPTER 5

Guarding Your Dreams

And Joseph dreamed a dream, and he told it his brethren: and they hated him yet the more.

Genesis 37:5

A s if it were not enough that Jacob doted on Joseph and favored him in so many ways, not long after Jacob gave Joseph his coat of many colors, Joseph began having dreams, dreams that he was convinced were from God and showed him having some divine destiny in the future. Worst of all, the dreams showed him ruling over his brothers and them having to bow down to him.

Joseph then told these dreams to his brothers, and this was more than they could bear. It had been bad enough that their earthly father had favored Joseph. Would their heavenly father, God, favor him too?

Joseph made some mistakes that furthered his brothers' hatred of him in this regard. When he began having the dreams, he should have kept them to himself. His brothers already hated him. Why antagonize them even more by telling them the dreams?

And the content of the dreams was terribly inflammatory. One day they would bow down to him. That was the last thing they wanted to hear. All of their lives they had watched him getting what they so longed for (their father's affections). And, for a very long time, they had understood the significance of the coat of many colors. That coat of royalty was Jacob's way of saying that although Joseph was the youngest, he wanted him to have firstborn rights. All of that, and now they were going to bow down to him? Forget that! He could die first as far as they were concerned.

They Hated Him Because of His Dreams

And his brethren said to him, Shalt thou indeed reign over us? or shalt thou indeed have dominion over us? And they hated him yet the more for his dreams, and for his words.

Genesis 37:8

Joseph was slow to learn his lesson. One needs only to look at the beginning of his story in the Bible to see just how naïve he was. Right at the beginning of Joseph's story, we're told that due to Jacob's blatant favoritism toward Joseph, his greater love for him and the gift of the coat of many colors *"they hated him, and could not speak peaceably unto him"* (Genesis 37:4). When Joseph had the first dream, we're told that in response to that dream, his brothers *"hated him yet the more"* (Verse 5).

It's interesting to note that it doesn't say they *would* not speak peaceably to him, but that they *could* not speak peaceably to him. The inward hurt felt by the brothers, due to Joseph's preferential treatment since his birth, was now manifesting itself outwardly. They didn't have a kind word for Joseph. There was no, "How you doing today, Joseph? Can big brother help you with anything?" There was no laughing and joking, as most brothers do. No, the brothers detested him. They spurned and ignored him. There was no discussion of any kind. Instead, they were mean to him, and they treated him treacherously.

What did Joseph do in light of his brothers' ill treatment of him? When he dreamed again, he told it to them in detail again.

In spite of the fact that they hated him, he still shared his second dream with them. Why would anyone share their dreams with people who not only don't like them; they hate them? How naïve can one be? Joseph failed to realize that there are times when dreams need to stay between you and God.

Dreams are important, and we need to learn to handle them properly. There are several important things to consider: First, when God gives you a dream, you may not fully understand it. That dream may well be tied to your purpose.

It often seems as if dreams are a lot like a puzzle. When you begin to put a puzzle together, the first thing you usually do is to find the four corner pieces. These are, in essence, the cornerstones on which the puzzle will rest.

After you find the four corner pieces, you begin to locate the straight edges (the border pieces), and put them into place. Finally, you begin to work on the picture in the puzzle.

Dreams are important, and we need to learn to handle them properly.

If you keep at it, eventually you'll see a partial picture appearing in one area. And, as you continue to work, you'll see another partial picture in some other area. In time, the whole picture begins to come into focus. Then you can see what the puzzle will look like when it's finished.

In the same way, God shows us bits and pieces of our lives. As we are faithful in one area, He reveals another piece. If God showed you everything about your life at once, you probably wouldn't be able to handle it. Also, before He shows you everything, He first has to test you and find you faithful. In time, He will show you more. Joseph knew that he would somehow rule one day, but little else.

Secondly, be careful whom you tell your dreams to. Joseph told too many and too much. Though Joseph was wrong to tell his brothers the dreams, the hatred they felt for him that day in response to his dreams was not all his fault. His brothers were carnal. There seems to be no indication that at that time in their lives any of the brothers was spiritually minded. And when a carnal mind hears spiritual truth, it doesn't seem to compute.

A carnal mind opposes spiritual revelation. It cannot see into the Spirit realm, and with its limited insight, it is often opposed to what God is saying. The carnal mind dwells only on the earthly realm.

You should also realize that when a carnal person knows you have a great purpose, they do not focus on the purpose. No. The carnal mind focuses on the person, not the purpose. It does not care how the dream might help people. All it sees is the glory, or recognition, the person will receive, and they resent it. After all, if anyone gets some glory, it should be them.

The word Joseph received through his dreams sounds awfully good, but since the carnal mind cannot receive the things of God, it all meant nothing to the brothers, except more glory for Joseph. What Joseph was telling them was a prophetic revelation of his future life, but he was sharing it with the wrong people. Be careful before whom you *"cast your pearls."* Jesus said:

> *Give not that which is holy unto the dogs, neither cast ye your pearls before swine, lest they trample them under their feet, and turn again and rend you.*

> Matthew 7:6

Dream Assassins

There are times when you cannot even tell your friends about your dreams. Some people seem to be your friends, but only until you begin to prosper and are elevated. Then they become jealous. Because of this, you may need to hide your dreams in your heart. Let them grow and be nourished. Keep them between you and God, rather than telling everyone else about them prematurely.

Why? Because many people are what I call dream assassins. They're on assignment from hell, they're armed and extremely dangerous, and they will stop at nothing to destroy the dreams of those who are chosen of God. They'll use any weapon at their disposal and adopt any tactic to achieve their desired end. Joseph's brothers were like that.

Although the dreams excited Joseph, they infuriated his brothers. If he had been wiser and had hidden his dreams in his heart, he might have been able to save himself a whole lot of grief and suffering. As it was, he only further angered his brothers and caused them to hate him all the more.

As I stated earlier, Joseph was clearly naïve. What older child wants to think of himself someday bowing down to a younger sibling? But another possibility is that Joseph was not so naïve. He was seventeen by now, and he surely understood what was going on in his household. It seems to me that there may have been a little streak of arrogance in him. He may have delighted in the dreams and the prospect of seeing his brothers bowing to him, and, if so, he couldn't help but tell them about it. That just pushed them further over the edge. It was like rubbing salt into their wounds.

Another thing that must have angered the other brothers was the surety of the dreams. Old Testament tradition held that if a dream was repeated two or more times, it was forever settled in heaven. That had to trouble them greatly. Established? They would see about that.

People Who Rise Against You Confirm Purpose in You

In one sense, it seems apparent that the brothers themselves believed the dreams had some substance. Usually, when some dreamer begins to make ridiculous claims, we discount them out rightly, and we may actually laugh at them. We surely don't take such people seriously.

People get stirred up only if they see you as a threat, only if they see potential in you. If you're nothing and nobody, they ignore you. Why should they care what you dream?

No one is jealous of a homeless person who lives on the streets. No one is jealous of someone who is a nobody. We're only jealous of those we think are destined to become great.

There was something about Joseph and his dreams that caused his brothers to take this all *very* seriously. Somehow they sensed that these dreams could actually come to pass. They would have cared less about the ramblings of a vain and foolish person, but what Joseph said disturbed them deeply. There was obviously something in Joseph's character that made them feel that his dreams just might come true.

This should be an encouragement to you when people come against you and try to stop your dreams. They may belittle you, but this should confirm the purpose and greatness in you. It should encourage you that others see your potential. That's why they're doing all they can to stop you.

It's surprising how many people there are like Joseph's brothers who will hate you because of your dreams. They get jealous, and then they try to dissuade you from believing your dream. They suggest that your dreams are not from God or that, for some reason or another, you're not worthy of them.

Even your close friends will try to throw cold water on your dreams. Why? Sometimes I think they just have a problem with people who succeed in life. Do something in life, anything of significance, and as soon as you accomplish it, you'll suddenly have enemies you never knew existed. It happens every time.

Those who seem to be your friends will suddenly take a step backward. Now, they're not so sure about you.

We don't like it when people treat us this way, and hopefully we won't treat others this way either. If there is any of this in you, ask God to remove it. Rejoice with your brothers or sisters in their successes, and don't be threatened by them. Any success they enjoy won't make you any less of a person. As they move up, you can move up with them, for it's all in the family.

The Power of Oneness

Commit yourself to being a dream supporter. When a friend gets a promotion, a new car, or new house, be happy for them. Refuse to allow a spirit of jealousy to control you. When your good friend arrives at church in a wonderful new outfit, looking like she has just stepped off the pages of *Vogue* magazine, be happy for her. Don't allow a spirit of jealousy to control you. Women, especially, are often guilty of this. We need to learn to support each other more, to be one with our fellow believers, because there's power in oneness.

At the tower of Babel, the people united for an evil purpose. Even then, God was impressed. He said:

Behold, the people is one, and they have all one language; and this they begin to do: and now nothing will be restrained from them, which they have imagined to do.

Genesis 11:6

Because there is such power in oneness, Satan will do everything he can to keep us from uniting and supporting each other. That's his job.

Although some women are guilty of jealous backbiting, most women are adept at creating a support system. Men, on the other hand, when widowed, remarry as quickly as possible. They usually don't enjoy the type of support system women build with each other. Yet support systems do lead to oneness.

We all need friends upon whom we can lean in difficult times. If we ever learn this concept of oneness, it will help all of us accomplish the purpose God has destined us for.

Now, back to Joseph. As I stated, part of the problem of the brothers was their carnal minds. Even today, when we tell people, "God told me … ," all sorts of red flags go up in their thinking. They don't like to hear those words, and they try to stop us before we can even get out what we want to say. The best policy is to keep our thoughts and dreams to ourselves unless God specifically shows us to tell them to someone spiritual enough to understand them. Let God establish your purpose, and then others will see it.

On the other hand, I encourage you: rather than being a dream assassin, become a dream preserver. Two women in the Bible demonstrate this point. One woman tried to kill a dream, while the other rose up to prevent it.

I Believe in Your Dream

The dream assassin was called Athaliah. She was the mother of King Ahaziah, and when he died, she decided that she wanted to become queen in his stead. To accomplish this, she would have to kill all of the royal grandchildren, the rightful heirs, and she set about to do just that.

This might have been accomplished, if it had not been for the cunning wisdom of another women, this one named Jehosheba. Jehosheba took one of the king's sons, Joash, and hid him, feeding and caring for him for six years, until he was old enough to assume the throne. The fact that Jehosheba hid and nourished the dream kept the throne of David alive in Israel, just as God had promised David many years before.

You can do that too—for yourself and for others. Protect your dreams from the Athaliahs around you, until the time for their fulfillment has come.

Elizabeth, the mother of John the Baptist, understood this need to protect a prophetic dream. She and Zechariah, her husband, were a godly couple, but they had waited for many years for a child, for she was barren. When she finally became pregnant, it almost seemed like a dream. She decided to hide herself for the next five months to give the child a chance to develop in her womb.

This was not an easy thing to do. She had been barren for so long that people had taken to calling her the "Barren One." Now that her curse of barrenness was finally broken, it would have been so tempting to begin telling it everywhere and to everyone. But Elizabeth was wiser than that. She held her peace and waited for the fulfillment, thus protecting the life of John the Baptist from anyone who might have wanted to do him harm.

Choose to be an Elizabeth, not an Athaliah. When God starts birthing something in you, hide it, give it a chance to take root and grow, and don't tell it to just everyone. Don't make Joseph's mistake.

Accepting Your Purpose without Man's Confirmation

Since Joseph knew what the attitude of his brothers was and knew that it was a risk to tell them his dreams, he may have been seeking acceptance by his brothers. All of us do that from time to time, and I have been guilty of it myself.

My husband, Chuck Singleton, is a great servant of God, both in and out of the pulpit, and I have learned a lot from him. Myself, I'm a Bible teacher. I love to take stories from the Word of God and use them to encourage people by showing them that the characters in those stories were people just like us. They went through the same things in life that we go through today. If they overcame, we can overcome, and I examine their stories to see how they did it.

When I first started preaching, and I went to minister at some church or event, I would come home and tell my husband about the acclamations people had made about my message. I later realized why I was doing this. I was hoping my husband would come to recognize what God had purposed in me and how God was using me to encourage people through His Word. Although I appreciated the words of others, what really mattered most was that my husband recognized and appreciated this gift of teaching God had placed in me. At times, we all have those insecurities to one degree or another.

I needn't have worried, for we have nothing to prove. We are whom God made us, and we owe no one an apology or an explanation. There are times that we have to be content to do as God has purposed, whether anyone favorably acknowledges our efforts or not.

Joseph didn't ask for people to bow down to him; God revealed that to him in the dreams. God called him to that position; so he had nothing to prove to his brothers. We must stop trying to please and influence people and concentrate on pleasing God.

This is Joseph's story, but God wants to make you a man or woman of dreams as well. And when men rise up against you and attempt to hinder the fulfillment of your dreams, God wants to help you hold on to Him and prevail, just as Joseph of old.

Expect God to speak to you, for He is in the habit of blessing those who have an expectation of blessing. Expectation demonstrates faith. Personally, I am always expecting God to bless me, and He never disappoints. He is the God of blessing, and I expect him to show His favor toward me on a regular basis.

> *...God wants to help you hold on to Him and prevail...*

The Price of Purpose

The truly odd thing about the reaction of Joseph's brothers to his dreams is that not one of them would have been willing to pay the price Joseph ultimately paid to see his dreams come true. Sure, they would have loved to stand in the palace, but they could not have been faithful in the process that was necessary to get Joseph there. They were not willing to go, but they resented him going. This is quite typical.

When Joseph told his father his dreams, Jacob didn't laugh. It did seem offensive to him that he would one day bow to Joseph, but he decided to keep the dreams in his heart and to meditate on their meaning. Since God had given Jacob himself revelations in dreams, he did not dismiss them as the ravings of a spoiled child, but realized that they were serious business.

What Lies Beneath

We live in southern California, and just last week, as I was writing this book, we experienced two horrific tragedies. After an unusually heavy rainstorm, an eleven-year-old boy fell into the San Antonio Creek and drowned. Then, the very next day, a mother and her young son fell victim to the same fate. As we listened to the news report in sorrow, we questioned why these people would get so close to such treacherous waters. Why would parents take such a chance?

And yet, as we continued to watch the unfolding news, we saw more families—mothers and fathers, with their small children—engaging in recreation at the very same spot. I grew angry as I watched this on television.

Then the newscaster came on and gave us some interesting information. In order to understand what he said, you must know something about southern California.

I have lived in southern California now for the past thirty-four years. One of the reasons I love the area so much is that the temperatures stay relatively warm throughout the year, and it rarely rains. (Rain between May and September is a rarity.) For the most part, any outdoor activity you plan during those five months will not be rained out. So, if you're like me, and don't like rain or cold, California is the place to be.

When I first came out here to California, I laughed at what they called rivers. Having grown up in Pennsylvania and Illinois, I knew what a real river looked like. Here in California, we don't have rivers. We have riverbeds, but there's no water in them most of the year. We have creeks, but they are just cute little streams in the foothills that you can easily wade through on a summer day or simply jump across.

Although we have a few rainstorms in October and November, the dry pattern continues for the most part until late December. But then January comes, and look out. From January through March, it seems that nature is making up for all the rain we don't get in May through September. The result is that everything floods. Houses slide down hills, freeways are closed because of rocks and boulders falling onto them, and many people are killed on the highways.

We had a particularly bad rainy season this year. Between December 27th and January 10th, fifteen days, we received seventeen inches of rain. Normally, we receive fifteen inches for the entire year. Thus far, it has been the rainiest season in southern California for the past one hundred and fifty years.

Because of all this rain, the riverbeds are now filled, and the creeks look like rushing rivers. And, since this is a phenomenon we don't often see, parents are bringing their families out for a time of recreation to look at the fast-moving water.

But what looks beautiful may not always be what it appears. The newscaster, as well as newspaper articles, informed us that the first boy and his fourteen-year-old cousin were playing in the creek, when powerful currents knocked both of them off of their feet. The older boy was able to force his way out, but the younger could not escape the water's grip. People standing by watched helplessly as he was swept downstream and finally drowned.

The next day, the second little boy and his mother both fell into the water. Jumping in to save them, the father was able to grab the little boy's hand for a brief second, but the water was moving so rapidly that it quickly pulled the boy from his grasp. Both mother and son drowned and were found a few days later a quarter mile downstream. I pray, in the name of Jesus, that this father will be able to move past that moment when his son's hand slipped from his grip, and not blame himself. The water was so treacherous that there was nothing he could do.

Contrary to popular myth, what you don't know can hurt you. What these people didn't know was that the swollen river, aside from moving rapidly, had a dangerous undercurrent. This was not immediately clear on the surface. The appearance of the water was deceiving, and this is why so many parents allowed their children to get close to it. And they paid the price. The treacherous undercurrent that lay beneath the surface of the water was so strong that it took the lives of three people.

In a way, this describes what was happening in the lives of Joseph's brothers. The intense jealousy and powerful hatred that was building up inside of them could not be seen, but it had now reached dangerous levels.

A Wounded Animal Is Dangerous

I like movies. I especially love animal movies. I can remember watching more than a few movies where there was a wounded bear, or animal of some kind, and a goodhearted farmer or ranger wanting to help the distressed animal. The problem is always that the animal is in so much pain that the farmer or ranger finds himself in danger from the very animal he so desperately wants to help.

People are not much different in this respect. Those who are critical, negative, or jealous hearted have often been so injured and wounded that they lash out at anyone trying to befriend them. Think about that the next time someone comes against you, and it will make a great difference in the way you respond to them.

As we look at this account, we first have to wonder what would cause ten older boys to want to murder their little brother? I'm the second of four children born to Joseph and Clotiel Palmer, and I have an older sister, Gloria, and two younger siblings, Eugene, who now goes by his given name Joseph, and Dianna. I can tell you that as I was growing up there were many times when both of these younger siblings got on my nerves so badly that I wanted to do them bodily harm. They would make me so angry.

My little sister Dianna was a spoiled brat, and my only brother was … well, let me just give you an example, and then you can fill in the blanks. On several occasions, when Gloria and I were watching television in the family room, Eugene would come in, pick up the remote control and change the channel. It didn't seem to matter to him that two people already had a prior claim to the television. Although Gloria and I both raised our voices in outrage, Eugene thought that he had done nothing wrong. He, in fact, thought that he had the right to the television set whenever he wanted it and no matter who was already watching it.

On one occasion, I got so angry that I wanted to beat him up. He had recently grown taller than me and, being a boy, had also gotten stronger than me. I waited for the right moment to get my revenge.

Eugene was a very sound sleeper. Once he had fallen asleep, it was nearly impossible to wake him up before morning. That night, about twelve o'clock, after he had been asleep for a few hours already, I got up and went to his bedside. (Since we were poor, all four of us slept in the same room.) I slapped him as hard as I could.

The next morning, I told him what I had done, but he had not been aware of it. Still, I was satisfied with my payback.

Growing up with sisters and brothers does bring conflict, and that conflict can lead to arguments and even outright fights. One receives some article that another one wants. One receives attention another one wants. One is forced to live in the shadow of another. These are common scenarios. Still, even in the midst of such hard times, in most families, love remains the underlying foundation. Because of this, we go only so far in our conflicts. And even when we want to choke a sibling, we don't. Underneath that sibling rivalry is something deeper and stronger—the underlying current of filial love.

From the very beginning of Joseph's story, we see that his brothers had an undercurrent affecting their lives too, but this was not an undercurrent of love.

Their undercurrent was one of hatred, fueled by their father's rejection and an atmosphere of constant jealousy and conflict. Finally, the generational problem of sibling rivalry caused their hatred to reach sufficient levels for them to act on it.

CHAPTER 6

When Your Purpose is Under Attack

And it came to pass, when Joseph was come unto his brethren, that they stript Joseph out of his coat, his coat of many colors that was on him; And they took him, and cast him into a pit: and the pit was empty, there was no water in it. And they sat down to eat bread.

Genesis 37:23-25

The Irony of the Coat

One day Jacob sent Joseph to Shechem to see about his brothers. The young men were shepherds and were often gone for long periods of time grazing their sheep. But when Joseph got to Shechem, his brothers were nowhere to be found. A man saw Joseph and informed him that the brothers had gone on to Dothan. Although Joseph could easily have gone back home, wanting to please his father and most likely see his brothers, he decided to go the additional thirteen miles to Dothan.

Not long after Joseph neared Dothan, he spotted his brothers in the distance. He was delighted. He had finally found them. Then, as he neared his brothers, he saw them coming toward him. In spite of the way they normally treated him, since they had not seen him for a while, he was hoping that they would be glad to see him. But it was not to be.

As Joseph drew near, his brothers saw his lone figure from a great distance, but they were able to recognize him because of his distinctive coat. That dreaded coat was an affront to them, and it brought back a flood of terrible memories.

The coat seemed to shout out: Daddy loved Joseph more than he loved them. It was a slap in the face from their father and from Joseph.

He had given Joseph his special coat, but he hadn't offered anything comparable to any of them. And, perhaps worst of all, in doing this, Jacob had made no apologies to his other sons, nor had he offered any excuses. His favoritism was blatant, and he didn't care who knew that he loved Joseph most. The coat was a symbol of that attitude, so they hated the coat. And they hated Joseph for wearing the coat. The coat caught their eye that day, greatly insulting them, and set in motion a family tragedy.

How could their father treat Joseph like he was some kind of king or prince, when he did nothing? They did all the work. But did they get a special coat? No! They hated that.

Every able man among them worked to sustain the family, but Joseph was not required to participate in that effort. Their time was spent working, while his time was spent with their father. That was infuriating to the other brothers.

For Joseph's part, as the second to youngest child in a family of twelve sons, he had grown up thinking that life revolved around him. Being Rachel's firstborn and only son for six years, as well as Jacob's son with his beloved Rachel, he was about as spoiled as a child could be. The coat said it all. The coat had become a symbol of their frustrations, a symbol of their disappointments, a symbol of their pain and when they saw that coat, they "lost it."

Still, it bears repeating again, the coat was very significant. It was a symbol of royalty, and it left no doubt about where Jacob wanted the power in the family to lie in the future. He favored Joseph, again and again, and he did it openly.

This blatant act of favoritism on Jacob's part had been almost sure to spark controversy and jealousy among the other brothers. With Jacob's history with Esau, he should have known that. Still, he did nothing to prevent this. Instead he turned his head and looked away from the obvious.

Parents can make a mistake in always allowing siblings to work out their own rivalries. In cases of open sibling opposition, parents need to keep a sharp eye out for signs of trouble and to pray for God's guidance as to whether or not they need to intervene at any given point.

The harsh feelings Joseph's brothers' felt had begun as simple jealousy. That jealousy had grown through the years until it had taken on a far more serious form—outright hatred. These brothers were no longer just jealous of Joseph; over the years the negative emotions had been building up. Now they hated him. They hated him because he was Rachel's son. They hated him because Jacob preferred him above them and made no apologies about that fact. They hated him because of his dreams. They hated him because he was such a spoiled tattletale, but by that time, they mostly hated him because of his special coat. That momentous day the hatred finally erupted.

When Hatred Erupts

As the brothers saw Joseph approaching that day, their rage went out of control, and they got into a huddle and planned a suitable line of attack. They would get rid of their little brother, the source of so much pain, once and for all. Their hatred was about to lead them to commit premeditated murder, and their lives would never be the same again.

As the brothers came closer, something seemed wrong. Joseph noticed a distortion in their faces. If they were happy to see him, their faces certainly didn't show it. What had he done now? He became apprehensive, and the huge smile on his face disappeared.

Closer the brothers came, and then, without warning, they suddenly rushed him. Attacking him, they threw him to the ground. Years of pent up anger overtook them, and they began to beat him. Blow after blow landed on poor Joseph.

"What are you doing?" he shouted. "Stop! Stop!" He was now on the ground. He felt a pain in his side as one of the brothers viciously kicked him. Then they started ripping off his coat.

It seemed like an eternity passed, but finally the beating stopped. Joseph was hurting so badly he couldn't get up. All he could do was lie on the ground in pain.

Then he felt himself being dragged along the ground. In a daze, he heard one of them say, "Let's not kill him; let's throw him into that pit." Abruptly someone picked him up and rudely pushed him down through an opening. Joseph felt himself falling into darkness. What a terrible experience that must have been!

It seemed as if Joseph was moving in slow motion when he abruptly hit the bottom. Sometime later he woke up. Where was he? It was dark, and he was lying in mud. He groped around and felt what had to be animal bones. He looked up. There was a light coming in from above. Joseph realized he must be in an abandoned well. He stood up and started yelling, "Let me out of here! Please, let me out of here!"

Joseph looked up again. This time he saw the outline of three heads peering down into the dried-up well and shouting, "Save your breath, Daddy's Boy! Nobody can hear you." They shouted other taunts too.

At some point, all dialogue ceased, the lid over the pit was closed, the light of the sun was extinguished, and Joseph was left alone with his own thoughts. His cries perhaps continued for some time afterward, but he eventually gave up and realized that his brothers had no intention whatsoever of helping him. He was on his own.

How could they not hear him? And how could they not respond? How could his brothers do such a terrible thing to him? How had their hatred grown to this point? At first, they'd had difficulty speaking peaceably to him, and he must have noticed that, but now this … ? This was extreme.

These were not children; they were grown men. And this was not child's play. This was deadly serious.

Exhausted from the effort, Joseph finally sat down and started crying. Why was this happening? How could his brothers have attacked him? What would happen to him now? As he sat there in frustration and grief, he began to ponder his fate.

The brothers, on the other hand were quite relieved. They were finally about to be rid of their hated little brother. There was no guilt and no remorse. Instead, they sat down together and had their afternoon meal.

What Had Just Happened?

Of the pit into which Joseph was thrown that day, the Scriptures say little, only that it was dry and that it was isolated. Reuben called it *"this pit that is in the wilderness"* (Genesis 37:22). Bible history tells us it was more of a well than a pit. Whatever the case, it was not a pleasant place that anyone would want to go, by force or otherwise. Joseph was forced into it.

How large was the pit? We don't know. What was it like? We don't know for sure. Most likely the pit contained discarded remains of dead animals. In those days abandoned wells were often used in this way. Joseph was probably in the company of some small rodents and insects.

How deep was it? We don't know that either. What we do know is that it was at least deep enough so that once Joseph was placed inside it, he couldn't get out of it by himself. I'm sure he must have tried, but his efforts were all futile. The brothers saw to that.

Was he injured when he hit the bottom? This we're not told either.

I can picture Joseph peering up, shouting desperately for his brothers to help him. Then, eventually, those shouts for help must have changed to threats of telling his father what they had done. They may have angrily retorted, "You're not telling anybody anything."

Whatever Joseph said that day, in shouts or sobs or otherwise, there was no positive response at all on the part of his brothers. They were determined to get rid of him in some way, as if doing this would somehow assuage their own pain.

Reuben to the Rescue

In his frustration and grief, Joseph probably didn't even realize exactly what had transpired that day. If he had known, he would have been even more troubled.

Joseph was unaware that his brothers had every intention of killing him and being rid of him once and for all. They had planned to kill him, throw his body into an abandoned pit so that it could not be found, and then they would devise some plan to tell their father—perhaps that Joseph had never reached the place They would think of something. No one would ever know what they had done.

Fortunately for Joseph, Reuben felt some responsibility for him. Whether he felt the same way about Joseph as the rest of them did or not didn't matter. As the oldest son, it was his responsibility to protect the lad.

Overhearing what the others were planning, he dissuaded them. He didn't want them to have the blood of their brother on their hands the rest of their lives, and he didn't want to have the lad's death on his conscience either. Rather than kill Joseph outright, he convinced them to throw Joseph into the pit alive and leave him there to die on his own.

At least that's what Reuben told the other brothers. In reality, his plan was to go back to the pit later, get Joseph out, and return him to their father. Unlike the others, Reuben wasn't anxious to see Joseph die. He had already put his birthright in jeopardy, when he was caught in an adulterous relationship with Bilhah, his father's concubine. Saving Joseph from the wrath of his brothers would perhaps help to soothe his father's wrath toward him. At the same time, he was not averse to seeing his little brother suffer a little. Maybe it would teach him a good lesson.

Joseph Had to Die!

As Joseph sat in that pit and pondered his future, his brothers debated among themselves what they should do with him. They were not about to let him go free. Their hated for him was too great, and they had waited too long for an opportunity to get revenge. Most of them were, again, in favor of killing him outrightly so that they could know with assurance that he was finally dead. If they just left him in the pit to die, it would be just their luck to have some shepherd come along looking for water and then rescue him.

That was a horrifying thought! Not only would Joseph be back, but also the full fierceness of their father's wrath would be on them for what they had done to his precious son. That very thought brought chills to them. No, there was no turning back now. Joseph had to die.

They continued to calmly eat their lunch, apparently feeling no remorse for what they had done and were about to do, and no grief over the separation from their brother. For sure, they still had no desire to show him mercy. As far as they were concerned, Joseph deserved this treatment; he had brought it on himself. Unsympathetic and callous, they were good and willing servants of Satan—dream assassins of the highest order.

Once I Thought I Was Wrong, But I Was Mistaken

It is not unusual for people to do wrong, only to justify that wrong by the actions of other people or circumstances. There always seems to be a good excuse for sin. "They" shouldn't have done that or said that.

You most likely know someone who feels it is *always* the other person's fault. No matter what the situation, they can never see *their* part in the wrong. These people are frustrating, to no end. Their logic makes no sense. No matter how hard you try to convince them of their part in the wrong, no matter how carefully planned your line of reasoning; they seem to have a mental block to the perception of any wrongdoing on their part. It still always ends up being someone else's fault. In the end, all you have to show for your efforts is a lot of wasted time.

> *It is not unusual for people to do wrong, only to justify that wrong by the actions of other people or circumstances.*

This attitude is often at the root of broken friendships and adulterous relationships. And you also frequently see this attitude with young people who are not getting good grades in school—due to lack of motivation on their part.

Having parented four sons, I've heard all of the excuses:

"You don't understand, Mom. Everybody gets bad grades in that teacher's class."

"That teacher doesn't know how to teach. Nobody understands what she's saying."

"That teacher just doesn't like me."

"That teacher is prejudiced."

Missed classes, late homework assignments, and lack of classroom participation seem to have nothing at all to do with bad grades. It's always the teacher's fault.

If you can see your reflection in these thoughts, please realize that you're a free moral agent, and no one can make you do anything. You make choices, and then you have to live with them. If you think you're always right and rarely find the need to apologize for some action, you're probably a prime example of someone who says, "Once, I thought I was wrong, but I was mistaken."

You need to ask God to open your eyes and let you see yourself for what you really are. When God eventually calls you into account, there will be no excuse. What will you say when you stand before Him?

Whether teen or adult, how is it that so many seem to have an appropriate excuse for their sin these days—no matter how evil and vicious their sin happens to be. Even in cases of something as evil as adultery, people make excuses and justify their behavior. There's a verse in the Bible that says:

This is the way of an adulterous woman: She eats and wipes her mouth, and says, "I have done no wickedness."

Proverbs 30:20, NKJ

In this case, the reference is to a woman who has entered into a sexual relationship with someone else's husband. Just as Joseph's brothers could sit down to eat lunch together with absolutely no sense of remorse or guilt, this woman can eat in peace and make the claim that she has done no wrong.

Nothing "Just Happens"

Women who do such things conveniently excuse their behavior by saying, "You don't understand how his wife treats him. He needs somebody to talk to. We didn't mean for this to happen. It just did" (or some other convenient excuse).

Let me take just a moment to address this. First, to the woman who truly did not plan for and does not want to be in an adulterous situation, let me encourage you. Aren't you tired of the guilt and the lies? End this thing now! Make the call, and get out!

Don't go to dinner to break it off. Definitely don't let him come over to tell him. Your flesh may turn on you. Realize that the man made a covenant before God with his wife, "for better or for worse, in sickness and in health, for richer or poorer, forsaking all others (that's you), till death us do part."

Let me ask you then: Is she still alive? Well, if she is, he just showed you that he's a liar.

In addition, because his wife is in covenant with him, once again before God, He is on her side. Oh my sister, breaking off the relationship with the man may cause you great pain, but at his home this very minute is a wife in great pain because she doesn't know what to do about the situation. At this point, it takes all her strength to stay sane and be strong for her children.

She knows that he's not home because he's with you, but what can she tell them when they ask her, "Where's Daddy?" Those children are in pain because their Mom is so sad. That household has no joy.

You may be right; the wife may be approaching him in the wrong way. But she doesn't know what to do. And you can't know about the times he purposely picked a fight so that he could leave and be with you.

I encourage you, if you are the woman of God you claim to be, send him back home, and pray for his marriage. Oh, and allow me to add, nothing "just happens." It happened because you didn't stop it.

You May Get What You Want, but Then You Won't Want What You Get

For those of you who are knowingly caught in this situation and simply refuse to get out, let me give you five reasons you should end the relationship. I pray that these will help you.

First, know that God calls you a *"strange woman"* (Proverbs 6:24). And, since that's what He calls you, I'll join Him. Strange woman, let me be blunt. It's none of your business how that man's wife is treating him. That is between him and his wife.

Second, don't be a fool. Have you talked to his wife? How do you know that his version of things is the true version? There are always two sides to every story. That man may just be trying to get you into bed. You may just be his flavor of the month.

Third, as far as him having someone to talk to, God already gave him someone to talk to ... his wife. If you back up and refuse to have a relationship with him, he may just go back to her. If he didn't have you to talk to, he might go home and talk to his wife—like he ought to do anyway.

Fourth, one day you'll probably realize why his wife was fussing all the time. Oh my sister, I pray that you don't cause this man to divorce his wife and marry you. If you do heartache, will follow. You always reap what you sow. You may get what you want, but then you won't want what you get. One day, you may be the wife dealing with the "other woman." Then, you'll come to realize why his wife fussed at him so much. You don't break God's laws; they break you.

After all, what makes you think that this man is above doing the same thing to you that he's doing right now to his wife? He's already shown you what he does during the hard times in marriage, and every marriage goes through them. If you marry him, you'll have some. Relationships are a little different when there are no bills, no children, and no responsibilities to deal with. Marriage is not just fun and sex.

The Line of Sin

Finally, you'll have to answer to God one day and face His judgment, and you will be without excuse. You're doing this on your own. No one can make you sin. There is a line of sin people willingly choose to step over. Circumstances, situations, and people can push you up to that line, but no one can push you over it. You have to willingly choose to step over that line.

Those who oppose God's will in other matters often seem to be just as defiant as this woman: *"I have done no wrong."* (Proverbs 30:20, NIV). One day, God will call you into account, and you will stand speechless before Him.

Wives May Need to Learn a Few Things From the Other Woman

For all of the wives who are saying, "Yes, you tell her," allow me to also tell you a few things. The other woman didn't get your husband by telling him how good for nothing he was. She didn't get him by looking just any old way. Wives may need to learn a few lessons from the other woman. The Bible tells us her strategy in Proverbs 5:1-23, 6:20-35, and 7:1-27.

This woman tells him how wonderful he is. Instead of turning her back to him at night or having a headache, she tells him, *"Come, let us take our fill of love until the morning"* (Proverbs 7:18). Translation: "I'm going to make love to you all night long."

Wives, I encourage you to learn to give your man the three A's: admiration, appreciation, and acceptance. Tell him what a wonderful man he is, or how strong or smart he is. Tell him you appreciate him going to work. Encourage him in his dreams. And finally, accept what you have. I guarantee you that if you don't want him, seven other women are standing in line who do. Men have egos that need to be fed. This is why we often hear about "the male ego." Be wise; give him a three-course meal.

I know what some of you are saying, "I go to work too, and he doesn't even thank me." Do you know what? If you keep that attitude, even if you don't lose your husband, you will eventually end up simply co-habitating with him.

Some of you, on the other hand, have responded positively to this encouragement, and immediately began thinking about the wonderful things you're going to tell your husband. But when you tried to think of positive things to say, you drew a blank. "Just give me a minute," you are thinking. "I'm sure there must be something good about this man." If this is your dilemma, after all your years of married life, let me give you a little help. Go back into the recesses of your mind and try to remember why you married him in the first place. It may take a minute, but it will come to you. Now, express these thoughts to him.

But be prepared, your man may go into a state of shock. I encouraged one friend to do this, and when she did, her husband said nothing. He just sat there in total silence. After a while, he asked her, "Are you talking to me?"

Above all give your man "the biggie," R-E-S-P-E-C-T. Every man wants and needs all that is represented by this seven-letter word.

Now, let's go back to Joseph.

Blowing Out the Other Man's Candle Will Not Make Yours Shine Any Brighter

When Joseph's brothers knowingly came against him, they didn't understand that eliminating Joseph would not make their father love them any more. Blowing out someone else's candle will not make yours shine any brighter. Eliminating someone else from competition does not automatically guarantee your success. Slandering someone else will not make you stand out any more. Maligning a fellow worker will never gain you a promotion.

Promotion does not come from any man, but from the Lord:

For promotion cometh neither from the east, nor from the west, nor from the south. But God is the judge: he putteth down one, and setteth up another.

Psalm 75:6-7

In addition, when Joseph's brothers stripped him of his coat and threw him into the pit, they genuinely believed that this would bring his dreams and destiny to an end. But the favor of God rested on Joseph, and although his brothers tried to strip him of that favor, they would eventually realize that the coat was not the favor. The coat was just a symbol of the favor. The favor of God was vested in the man, and nothing these jealous brothers could do would change that fact.

They were, therefore, limited in what they could do to Joseph. They had the power to strip him of his coat, and they did that. But they did not have the power to strip him of the favor that was upon his life.

People Can Delay Your Dreams, but They Cannot Stop Them

The brothers also failed to remember the fact that God had given Joseph the dream on two different occasions. This showed that his destiny had been sealed in the heavenlies. God was now responsible to protect that destiny. Therefore, unbeknownst to them, Joseph could not be killed. He had to fulfill his God-purposed destiny. Because He knew what the brothers would do that day, the plan to preserve Joseph's life had already been set into motion by His hand.

As the brothers discussed the murder of their little brother, Judah looked up and saw a caravan of Ishmaelite traders approaching from a distance. With that, a plan began to form in his mind. They could sell Joseph into slavery. Not only would they be rid of him, but also they could make a profit in the process.

Due to their brutal existence, the life of the average slave was very short. The hard manual labor, combined with a lack of proper nutrition and a lack of medical attention for sicknesses, often sent slaves to an early grave. Joseph would be dead soon enough, but not by their hand. Judah shared his plan with his brothers, and they reluctantly agreed to it.

Men may strip you of things, or even of titles or prestige, but they cannot go deeper— unless you let them.

Do you really believe that the caravan just "happened" to come along at that particular moment? Of course it didn't. God was in control. It was not within the brothers' power to kill Joseph. God still had a purpose for him. That purpose, as we will see, was in Egypt, so God was simply allowing Joseph to be positioned for purpose.

As painful as it might have been for Joseph to be stripped of his coat, God would eventually use it. Remember, *"all things work together for good to those who love God, to those who are the called according to His purpose"* (Romans 8:28, NKJ). No man has power to hurt us when we're in God. None can do anything to us that God does not permit them to do. Therefore, if He permits a thing, we can know that God will use this for our good.

Men may strip you of things, or even of titles or prestige, but they cannot go deeper—unless you let them. Only God has the power to grant you His favor, and only God has the power to remove that favor from you.

CHAPTER 7

Positioned for Purpose

And they drew and lifted up Joseph out of the pit, and sold Joseph to the Ishmeelites for twenty pieces of silver: and they brought Joseph into Egypt.

Genesis 37:28

After some undetermined period of time, Joseph was pulled from the pit. How deeply relieved he must have been! Surely God had heard his cries! Surely his brothers had repented of their wrong attitude! He was overjoyed, and his tears of despair suddenly turned into tears of gratitude. He was thanking God and thanking his brothers at the same time.

The Next Crisis

But Joseph's joy was short-lived. Just as suddenly as he had been pulled from the pit, he was handed over to a group of men waiting nearby with their camels. These men proceeded to place him in chains and rudely lead him away.

Wait a minute! Who were these men? What were they doing to him? Where were they taking him? Why was this happening? There were so many questions and seemingly no answers.

It would have been nice to think that Joseph had remained calm and collected through all of this, but that simply wasn't the case. He was human, after all, just like you and me. Plus, he was only seventeen years old. No, he didn't go quietly at all. Joseph cried out to his brothers to help him, and he pleaded with them not to sell him. They remained silent. Even as he cried out to them and reached desperately for them, they turned a deaf ear. He was understandably in great distress, and he let that be known.

As the slave traders dragged him away, Joseph fought to see his brothers as long as he possibly could and continued to cry out for their help long after they could hear him. Then, slowly, they began to recede into the distance, and after a while, they were gone.

The brothers were actually enjoying the sight of him being in such despair. Was he mistaken, or had they been smiling as he finally vanished from their sight? He could not know it, but they were now twenty pieces of silver richer, and they were even then pondering how they could best spend their newfound riches.

As he disappeared into the distance, the Scriptures record:

And his brethren were content.

Genesis 37:27

These brothers were very happy with themselves. They had cleverly killed two birds with one stone. They had rid themselves of the greatest thorn in their existence, and, at the same time, enriched themselves. Now, with Joseph out of the way, surely Jacob would love them and pay them some attention, as he should have all along—or so they considered. The uppermost thought in their minds was that now their lives would surely be better.

As for Joseph, until this day he had lived a life of ease. Now he was being sold into an uncertain future. We can only imagine how we might have reacted under these same circumstances.

How terrible it must have been for Joseph that his own brothers were not moved by his cries, or if they were, it was not enough to overcome their greed and the anger they felt for him! Despite his every plea for help, they sold him anyway. Apparently, he meant absolutely nothing to them.

How could he be expected to cope with the idea of being sold into slavery— and not just sold into slavery, but sold by his own brothers? The thought of it is mind-boggling.

What Was Happening?

Just that quickly, the boy who had been destined for greatness and had long been robed in royal splendor as a sign of it, now found himself bound and being led helplessly away. What was happening? And why?

One thing is sure. Joseph was again alone and helpless, and his future suddenly seemed totally out of his control. He was now among uncouth slave traders who cared nothing for his comfort and safety.

What Had Joseph Done Wrong?

As Joseph walked in chains to Egypt, he must have mulled over in his mind the events of the day, playing and replaying them over and over again, hoping to see where he had gone wrong. What had he done to bring this upon himself?

He had been so happy when he finally located his brothers, and as he was coming over the last hill toward them, I imagine that he had begun to rehearse in his mind what he would say. "Father sent me to see how you're doing." He was perhaps hoping that his willingness to come so far to find them might now end the animosity they felt for him.

He was surely expecting nothing less than smiles and hugs from them in return. How could he have anticipated what would greet him instead? Could he have ever considered in his wildest dreams that his brothers would try to do him physical harm?

But now that he had time to think about it, he may have realized that as he was arriving that day, there had been a strange feeling in the air. If he had looked closer, could he have seen the fire in his brothers' eyes and the snarl on their lips?

Something had hung in the air that day so thick that you could cut it. But what was it? Why had he not been able to identify it before? Why had his own blood brothers suddenly turned into a pack of snarling and ravenous wolves, turning on him and trying to do him harm?

If he had been more sensitive, could he have realized what was in their hearts as they began to advance on him and attack him menacingly? Should he have resisted more? Could he have outrun them if he had tried harder?

Having members of your own family turn on you and try to do you harm is a very painful experience for anyone. There is no pain quite like family pain, and nobody can get to you quite like another family member can.

I still remember the emptiness I saw in the eyes of a grocery store clerk one day, many years ago, as she rang up my order. She was not crying, yet the pain in her eyes was so very apparent that it was troubling. I asked her what was wrong. God had ordained this encountered so that no one was behind me, and she began to recount her story.

The clerk's sister, whom she had not seen for some time, was coming to town to visit. For most people, this would have been a happy occasion, but, in her case, the very thought of it brought pain. Many years earlier her sister had had an affair with her husband. The husband had divorced her and married her sister.

Now her sister and her former husband were returning to town to attend a birthday celebration for their mother. The clerk had fervently objected, as had other members of the family. The mother had been so hurt by the behavior of her daughter that the subject still brought her much pain.

The family had expressed to the couple that their presence was not wanted. It would only bring further grief to them on what should be a joyous occasion for their mother. Even if they returned to visit, attending the party was simply out of the question.

Still, the offending couple refused to change their minds. They felt that the family should "get over it" and be happy for them. (Remember, *"she eats, and wipes her mouth, and says, 'I have done no wrong'"* (Proverbs 30:20, NRS). The store clerk was hurt, angry, and bitter, and yet she still had to hold it together while she rang up my groceries. In spite of her sorrowful situation, she knew she still had to keep living.

I cannot imagine the agony I would experience from any woman taking my husband, but especially if one of my own sisters did it. Tears are streaming from my eyes even now as I type this story.

I told the clerk that I would pray for her, and, although that was fifteen years ago; I still pray for her to this day. I trust that she has been able to get past that season and that God gave her a man who would appreciate her.

Joseph, like the grocery store clerk, was greatly hurting and trying desperately to understand it all.

"If Only"

Over and over he must have pondered what might have happened had he been more observant. He probably was angry with himself for failing to see what seemed to be obvious now. "If only I had paid more attention, I could have stopped this." His mind was a swirl of emotions.

At some point you have to come to peace with yourself.

How had he missed the signs of their increasing hatred in recent days and weeks? How had he been oblivious to the fact that it was reaching the boiling point?

Satan is a master at torment, and he is keen on blaming us for everything that happens—whether we had anything to do with it or not. If we don't blame ourselves, he whispers, we need to place the blame somewhere. This happens so often when tragedies occur. "If only they hadn't done that," "If only I had done this," "If only I hadn't said that," "If only I had left earlier," "If only I had gone a different way," "If only I had stopped and done this," "If only … " "If only …" "If only …"

People can stay in the place of "if only" for long periods of time while they blame themselves, others, or even God. At some point you have to come to peace with yourself. Maybe it would have been better if you had done it differently, but the reality is that you didn't. What a wonderful thing it would be if we could go back and change the past, but the harsh reality is that we can't. As much as we wish we could, we cannot do it. We cannot even go back one hour.

Things happen in life, and sometimes there is no one to blame. Things somehow get out of our control. The rain falls on everybody—the just and the unjust alike.

The Pit as the Place of Purpose

Since the pit was God's place of purpose for Joseph at the moment, he probably could not have escaped it, regardless of what he had done. But right now he didn't know that. Whatever the case, he was headed to Egypt.

Now Joseph was no doubt sorry that he had told the brothers his dreams. Like many of us, he was learning his lesson the hard way. He now wished that he had been more sensitive to their feelings and that he had kept his thoughts and feelings to himself. If they couldn't handle the truth about his destiny, he should just have kept it inside, pondering on it in his heart and allowing time to declare it openly. That's what he should have done. Now he knew it, but it was too late.

Learning to Depend upon God

What had happened had happened, and now Joseph just needed to make the best of it somehow. He was hurting, but he needed to hold on through his pain and cling to his dream. Desperately, somehow he was able to do that.

Why was he here? Had God left him? Was his destiny lost?

What he may not have realized in that moment was that if he could just hold on to God through every pain that came to him, the experiences ahead, and indeed this current experience, God would use these all to do something very positive for him, and make him a better person. For one thing, slavery would definitely cause him to grow up fast, and in the process it would teach him a lot about God. Before it was over, he would surely know the Lord a lot better.

For another thing, being alone with no one to talk to would teach him to turn to the Lord, not to people. This would save him a lot of time and energy in the future. Depending on other people is often a terrible waste of time. We all need to learn to go directly to God. He never fails.

What Was Jacob's Role in All of This?

As the caravan made it's way to Egypt, Joseph had to have passed by Hebron in the distance. As he looked over the rolling hills toward his father's tents, his thoughts must have gone to his father. Did he have any idea, when he had sent Joseph to meet his older brothers that they would try to harm him? And if not, then why not?

The other sons were old enough that they should have been trustworthy, but if Jacob had known what was in their hearts, he surely would never have sent Joseph to meet them that day, thus placing him in harm's way.

The sad truth is that Jacob was not a very wise parent, and I'm convinced that God had to take Joseph out of Jacob's house in order to make him the man He wanted him to be. Joseph would have eventually achieved his purpose if he had remained in his father's house, but at the very least, it would have taken him much longer to accomplish it. At home, he had been sheltered and never had to lift a finger. Now, he would have to endure a painful separation from his father and the rigors of slavery, but it would help him to mature as a person.

Modern parents do everything within their power to keep their children from suffering as they did in their childhood, and yet by sheltering them, we may actually be doing them harm. We are who we are today because of the experiences we've been through, and how can our children have these experiences if they're always protected?

We were not handed everything we wanted. We had to work for it, and if we couldn't work for it, we did without. We learned to make many of the things we needed. We made our own toys and learned how to entertain ourselves. We played baseball with a broomstick for a bat, and we had all kinds of fun with a big cardboard box. We seemed to appreciate the simple things of life.

Today, children have so many things that they can't decide what to play with first, and still they don't seem to appreciate how very good their life is. Personally, I don't believe it's healthy to have everything handed to you on a silver platter. Those who have to be concerned about their daily needs also seem to be more apt to seek God.

I can remember eating mayonnaise sandwiches as a child. When we had lettuce to put on them, we thought we were rich. We never even missed not having any meat to use.

I remember when we only had two pairs of shoes, one for everyday and another for special occasions. I remember those everyday shoes wearing out too soon and us having to put cardboard insoles in them to block the holes in the soles. We were happy just to have shoes to wear, and we would never have thought of asking our parents for another pair. That was unthinkable. Now most of us have closets full of shoes, one or more pairs in every color.

But all of that sacrifice didn't kill us. God used it to develop honesty and integrity in us. It gave us character. It caused us to appreciate Him and what

He has done for us. And as life improved, we could rejoice, because we knew where God had brought us from. It all had a healthy purpose.

Why Did He Have to Be Stripped?

Suddenly, without his beloved coat, Joseph somehow felt naked. Why had they ripped off the coat that meant so much to him and signified so much to others? It had spoken to him of security and safety. Now it was gone, everything was gone—father, family, friends, home, and the coat. Joseph felt very vulnerable.

You, too, may know what it feels like to be stripped. And, if it hasn't yet happened to you, keep on living long enough, and it will. There's always a stripping of some sort that must take place in each of our lives if we are to be used of God. And He does want to use every one of us. His desire is that we make our mark on this world, affecting the people and situations around us for good.

When you eventually die (and we all die at some point), will people say only that you lived and then you died with nothing in between? If so, that's not much of a legacy, is it! You were born, and you will die, but what of the period in between?

For my part, I want people to know that Charlyn Michelle Palmer Singleton walked this earth, not for the sake of my ego, but because I want to impact the world around me for God. I'm sure that Joseph felt the same way.

And, just as Joseph had to pass through the pit, we also have to experience some pain in life to get where we're going. To get to where I am today, I've had to suffer some, and I know that I'll suffer more in the days ahead, because with each step we take, there come new testings. Get ready to be tested, and know that when it comes, it's for the Lord's glory.

When Joseph's brothers stripped him of his coat, this was just the first of several strippings that would take place in his lifetime. If, each time it happened, he could refuse to become bitter and angry, God would enlarge him through this.

Where Was God In All of This?

As Joseph walked to Egypt that day, I cannot help but believe that he must have questioned God's role in all of this. Why had God not intervened on his behalf? Why had He allowed this terrible thing to happen? "Doesn't He love me anymore?" he must have wondered.

Yet, as Joseph was being led in shackles to Egypt, God was with him, just as He had been with him in his father's house, and just as He had been with him it the pit. God's presence with him had not diminished in any way.

We can never allow ourselves to think that God is with us only when things are going well and people love us. No, God is with us in the good times and in the bad. He allows various people—even friends, family members, and associates—to oppose us while we're on our way to fulfilling His purpose for our lives. It's all part of the process.

That may not make it any easier to bear or any less hurtful, but it is something to hold on to. God is Jehovah Shammah, the God who is present. Even though you cannot see Him, He's right there with you.

You will be attacked, so get ready for that. And when you are attacked, God may not intervene and rescue you immediately. People will do you wrong and seemingly get away with it. They will treat you cruelly and seem to suffer no apparent consequences for what they have done. The wicked sometimes seem to prosper, while the righteous seem to languish in dishonor.

Part of this is that God chooses not to violate man's free will. That's how we all got into trouble in the first place in the Garden of Eden. Adam made wrong choices, and God chose not to violate his free will. In the same way, He allowed Joseph's brothers to do what they had so carefully crafted in their minds to do.

When Hell Wars Against Heaven's Plans

Even as his brothers were beating, stripping, and selling Joseph, God had a plan of His own. He would use the brothers' fierce behavior for Joseph's good. What the brothers were doing played into His hands and His plans.

Oh yes, Satan was doing his part too. In his dreams, Joseph had seen his brothers and his father bowing to him, and that meant that he would become very great indeed. (Family is always the last one to recognize talents.) But this would not happen without a fight. Hell always wars against heaven's plans and purposes for you. Promotion rarely comes without a struggle. Hell is at war right now against your prayers, against your purpose, and against your destiny.

Slavery Was Not a Part of the Dream

So had his brothers postponed, or perhaps totally obliterated, his dreams? Perhaps the worst thing about Joseph's situation was that it all seemed contrary to the dreams. In his dreams, he had not seen a pit. In his dreams he had not seen chains, and he had not seen the attack of his brothers.

When God gives you a dream, hold on to it, even if everything that's currently happening in your life seems to be going against that dream.

Many of us can identify with Joseph. Although God speaks to us very specifically—of marriages being restored, children coming back to Him, ministries being imparted, and great works being accomplished through us, what actually happens in our daily lives often seems totally contrary to what He has promised. Why is it that our dreams sometimes seem not only to not be coming true, but the very opposite seems to be happening? "What's happening?" we wonder, "And why?"

We have a lot to learn. God's Word is sure, but He fulfills it in His own time, and in His own way. Learn to wait patiently for Him. He has a reason for every delay.

Never Doubt in Darkness

When God gives you a dream, hold on to it, even if everything that's currently happening in your life seems to be going against that dream. It might appear as if God has forgotten the dream, but He never forgets, and you must not forget either.

I encourage you to hold to the dream so tightly that it can never escape. No matter what happens in the future, cling to that dream. No matter what circumstances come your way, cling to that dream. No matter what other people say, cling to that dream.

God has promised you some amazing things. They are so amazing that sometimes you may have difficulty believing them yourself. As time passes and your dream has not been fulfilled, it becomes easier and easier to let it go and to think that it will never come to pass.

"Maybe I was mistaken," you begin to think. "Was that really God?" Well, at the time He spoke to you, you knew who was speaking. What He was saying then seemed very clear, and you knew that it was for you. Now, the fact that some time has gone by without the fulfillment of the dream does not change anything. God knows what the perfect timing of all things is, and He is never late. You must believe in your own dreams and hold on to them, and *never doubt in darkness what God has shown you in the light.*

Between the time of the dream and the time of its fulfillment, there must come a time of serious preparation. If the dream has not yet been fulfilled, then you can know that you're still in the preparation process for it.

Subconscious "Haters"

We all need to come to the place that we decide not to entrust our dreams to others. Even some of those who attend church services are not there to worship the Lord. Satan has his emissaries in church too. And not everyone who claims to be your friend actually is your friend. Because of the ulterior motives behind their friendship, some are what the young people now call "haters." They'll presently have a problem with your success. In general, they resent you or anyone else who equals them in position, popularity, possessions, or anything else.

At the same time, some of your "friends" are as much a friend as they know how to be. But they, too, may not be able to handle victory, prosperity, and promotion in your life and not be consumed by envy and jealousy.

Because of this, recognize that there are times when you have to protect your dream from your friends. Sometimes, something inside of people causes them to have problems with those who achieve possessions or position, even if they are their friends. They may not even understand why they have such a hard time rejoicing in their friend's accomplishment. And this may actually bother them, but they don't know what to do about it. In reality, they are happy for their friend, but something on the inside makes them hold back their praise, or change the subject when others are applauding the friend's achievement. At times, they may even begin to avoid those friends. These emotions may be due to something in their childhood, they may be due to the fact their own dreams seem to be on hold, or they may even be due to demonic influence.

This very morning, as I was writing this, my friend, Tracy Bennett, called to tell me that she had passed her real estate exam. I was thrilled. Tracy had only recently gotten promoted to the position of Director of the Kidney Stone Center at Pomona Valley Hospital. Now she had passed her real estate exam. And she was also in the final phase of completing another degree. Over the years, Tracy had shared some of her dreams with me, and I was not only proud of her; I was also delighted to see that she was on her way to fulfilling these.

I could be happy with Tracy for three reasons. (1) She had been a faithful friend for years, and I loved her dearly, (2) I had completed many of my own goals and was on my way to finishing my first book (a dream I had held in my heart for nineteen years, and (3) Tracy had been one of my most enthusiastic supporters.

If you pray and ask God to open doors of destiny for you, you'll not have to envy others when He opens doors for them. I don't have to envy or be jealous of Tracy because I'm in the process of accomplishing some of my own dreams.

If you find yourself in this dilemma, understand what's going on. Sometimes, someone just being your friend is not enough. Often, when people see others achieving dreams, if they're not doing something themselves, this can bring about feelings of envy. And, if your friends don't support your dreams, you may have difficulty supporting theirs.

Also, if you find yourself in this predicament, also realize that there's a distinct possibility that these feelings may be from Satan. Have you ever heard of someone with a critical spirit? There are also spirits of jealousy, envy, anger, and bitterness, etc. These demonic influences are always looking for someone to whom they can whisper their poison, and they're looking for someone who will allow these words to take root in their soul. Such demonic forces will do anything to meet their desired goals.

The Bible says, *"The spirits of the prophet are subject to the control of the prophets"* (1 Corinthians 14:32, NIV). In other words, what goes on inside you is under your control. Pray and ask God to give you joy over another person's success, whether they happen to be a friend or not. If you're a Christian, you have this power given to you as a believer. Rebuke that spirit in the name of Jesus. Determine that you will rejoice with your friend's success. Resist the devil, and he will flee from you.

The Importance of Suffering

Although Joseph was far from his father's house, and was getting farther from it by the minute, he was still in his place of purpose. God had a purpose for Joseph before he was born, and that purpose was to be fulfilled in Egypt. Although his revelation did not match his situation, God had a promised end in sight. Joseph's purpose was in Egypt, and so God had allowed his brothers to provide the transportation for him to get there.

Isn't life strange? In sending Joseph to Egypt, the brothers definitely had evil in mind. These young men had attacked, stripped, and sold him with the intention of stopping his dream. But not only did they not stop Joseph's dream from coming to fruition; what they did was help Joseph to get to his place of purpose. And by doing this, their hatred and rejection of Joseph actually ended up accelerating his purpose.

God had destined Joseph for leadership. But leaders must know what it means to suffer. They must know about standing alone. There are times that they must act without the confirmation of others. Leaders cannot be creampuffs.

Joseph had led a creampuff life in Jacob's house. He was spoiled and sheltered. In his father's house, he was anything but a leader. Joseph needed to learn to suffer, and he needed to be out of Jacob's house to fulfill his purpose.

Would Jacob have given his consent for Joseph to travel to Egypt to look for work? Never! Would he ever have agreed to Joseph doing manual labor in the house of an unbeliever? Never! Would he ever have stood by while Joseph sat in a prison cell overlooked and unappreciated? Never! So God had no choice. It had to be done this way.

God knew what He was doing. The men of the caravan may have been slave traders, but God used their wrong desires to accomplish His righteous ones. He needed Joseph to get down to Egypt, and his brothers helped to facilitate that need.

CHAPTER 8

Purpose Delayed

We're not given any information about Joseph's trip to Egypt. It must have been a nightmare for him. This was the first time he had been separated from his father. The first few days, at least, he must have been sore from the attack of his brothers. Walking such a distance on foot in chains had to be difficult—physically and emotionally. But more than that, these men surely treated Joseph harshly. He was now a common slave.

It's not difficult to imagine the torments that were raging in Joseph's mind, the lies Satan was telling him, and the struggle between his faith and the facts of his reality. He had been born to rule. He knew that. Why, then, was he now in bondage? That didn't seem to make sense. Of course, in time it would.

Deceit Revisited

It seems certain that Joseph thought of his father a great deal during his trip to Egypt and his ordeal at the slave auction, and indeed, during the days and weeks to come. The two of them had been inseparable, and Joseph had become almost totally dependant upon his father. Being so far from Jacob had to be, for Joseph, a great part of the loss he was now suffering. What Joseph could not know was that Jacob was experiencing his own period of intense grief. Even then, back home, a tragic scene was unfolding.

When the brothers returned home, it must have been with great trepidation about what they would tell their father and what his reaction would be. Up to now, their plan had worked. The caravan had been an extra bonus. Everything was working together, seemingly without repercussion. This caused them to become more and more confident. And now they were ready for the next step.

They had hurt their brother, and he deserved it, and they were about to hurt their father, and he deserved it too. Yet, these young men had no idea how deeply their actions would wound their father. As far as they were concerned, Joseph was dead for all intent and purpose. With this blow, a part of Jacob was about to die too.

Rather than lying to Jacob, the brothers decided to present him with the bloodied coat and let him draw his own conclusions—that wild animals had devoured Joseph. When they arrived home, they went to Jacob and told him they had found the torn coat. They asked him if it was the coat of Joseph? And it worked perfectly:

And he ... said, It is my son's coat; an evil beast hath devoured him; Joseph is without doubt rent in pieces. And Jacob rent his clothes, and put sackcloth upon his loins, and mourned for his son many days. And all his sons and all his daughters rose up to comfort him; but he refused to be comforted; and he said, For I will go down into the grave unto my son mourning. Thus his father wept for him.

Genesis 37:33-35

When Jacob saw the coat, he "lost it" He was beside himself.

No! Not Joseph! Not his beloved Joseph!

My Joseph ... attacked by wild animals ...eaten. No!

What a heartbreaking scene it was! Only someone who has suffered such a painful loss could understand the agonizing, unbearable heartache Jacob was feeling in those moments. It is bad enough to have your child die, but when your child dies tragically, it multiplies the pain.

The terrifying manner in which Joseph died, no doubt, tormented Jacob. Over and over, I'm sure, he pictured his beloved son being attacked by wolves or some other wild beasts. And Jacob could only imagine the fear his son felt as he ran for his life, only to have the beasts catch up to him, kill him, and then eat him. The picture was horrifying, and Jacob could not get the images out of his mind.

I still remember the young teenager back East who was killed and partially eaten at a zoo some years ago. He and his friend had skipped school that day, gone to the zoo, and climbed down into an area occupied by some sleeping polar bears. Then something had awakened the bears, and one of them went after the two boys.

The boys ran, and one of them was able to climb out, but the mother bear, grabbing the other boy by the leg, dragged him into her den and killed him. We heard later that the authorities had killed the bear and removed the boy's partial remains from her stomach.

Even though I heard that report many years ago, the thought of it still haunts me to this day. I remember thinking that I hoped he fainted from fright before the bear had killed him. Having young children of my own, I could only imagine that bear coming closer and closer to the boy, opening her mouth, and then those ferocious teeth tearing into him.

It was the stuff of horror movies, and these things are not supposed to happen in real life. But in Jacob's case, it did happen in real life. His boy was dead, and he had died violently.

In addition to the way Joseph died, since the death of Rachel, Jacob's whole life had been wrapped up in Joseph, and now he, too, was gone forever. Rachel was gone, and now Joseph was gone. Jacob found this to be inconceivable, and he was thus inconsolable: *"He refused to be comforted"* (Genesis 37:35).

Joseph had not been the only one to believe that he had a great future. Jacob had believed it for a very long time now. He had seen something in his son that had led him to give the lad the special coat. He had been so happy that out of the chaos of his confused household, such a fine specimen had emerged. Now Joseph was gone, and only the bloody coat was left as a reminder of what might have been. The sight of that coat must have torn Jacob to pieces for a long time to come.

How could he have been so wrong about Joseph? Jacob now experienced his own period of extreme testing. Were it not for the fact that this story is about Joseph, no doubt the details of Jacob's ordeal would be given a more prominent place. Jacob's ordeal, although different from that of Joseph, was nonetheless a very difficult one.

Reaping the Whirlwind

One cannot help but remember the day Jacob had deceived his father many years before. This practice of deceit had come full circle, and now his sons were practicing the same deceit on him. He had lied to his father concerning Esau, pretending he was his brother. Now his sons were lying to him about their brother. The Bible tells us you *"sow the wind, and reap the whirlwind"* (Hosea 8:7, NIV). Jacob was now caught up in his own private storm of grief, and he would stay there for many, many years.

On the brothers' part, how could they have known their father would be so grief stricken? The twenty pieces of silver no longer looked so good, and Joseph no longer looked so bad. Somewhere deep down they now actually missed him and shared a small bit of grief themselves. But it was too late now. Joseph was gone. He would be dead in a few short years. It was done.

With the thought that there was nothing more they could do on the outside, the guilt and grief of it all settled into their hearts. That guilt would haunt them for years to come.

Getting To the Place of Purpose

Of course, Joseph didn't know it yet, but Egypt was his place of purpose. It may have seemed like a place of torment to him at the time, but all he had to do was remain faithful, and he would be on his way to purpose. That would become clear only with time.

For now, all he knew was that he was a slave, separated from his family, far from his loving father and the grave of his long-dead mother. And there was absolutely no one he could call on here. He was alone with God. Who else could he ask to get him out of this awful place?

We often experience this same thing:

"Who can I ask to help me pay these urgent bills?"

"Who can I turn to now when my children are acting like heathens?"

"Who can I go to for healing now that the doctors have given me very little hope?"

"Who can I turn to now that my boss has mistreated me and deprived me of a merited raise or promotion?"

"Who can I go to now that the bank has denied by home loan?"

People have a way of becoming prayer warriors during times of desperation. When we realize that no one can help us and we cannot help ourselves, we usually then turn to God. Although it doesn't feel very good at the time, actually being in a place where you're alone can be a good thing. These are the occasions in which we finally find the time to be alone with God.

Christians Are Also Guilty

God will use a whole variety of people to get us to our place of purpose. Sometimes it will seem as if these people want to do anything but help us. And, you're right, they don't. Yet, in spite of their motives and actions, and in spite of the fact that they may be evil and jealous, and are doing all they can to push you down, God still uses these people. There are no accidents in the Christian life.

All Joseph Had Now Was His Dreams

All Joseph had now was his dreams. God had shown him that they were established, by giving them to him two times, and yet they were not happening. They had seemed so real, and he had been so sure that they would come to pass. Now, some part of him tried to hold on to the hope that the dreams were real and that God had really given them.

Many of us, like Joseph, are trying to hold on to our dreams. It's not that we don't remember them. Most of us do remember dreams that come from God. Those dreams are so vivid that we still remember what the weather was like the day He spoke to us, what we had on, and what song was being sung in a given church service. But sometimes reality makes it hard to hold on to those dreams. I encourage you not to look at the circumstances or situations. Hold on to your dream. When God speaks a word, it will come to fruition. When and where it will happen we cannot say. All we can do is hold on and be faithful in the meantime.

God was preparing Joseph for leadership, for every leader must first know how to follow. Every supervisor must know well the positions he will supervise. Otherwise, how can he supervise them?

Joseph needed to develop the spirit of the servant that had long been in him. Although the gift was already inside, because he had no opportunity to serve, the gift had not been developed. That and other gifts needed to be developed and sharpened before God could use Joseph to accomplish the great purpose He had destined him to fulfill.

Joseph had to learn that life was not all about him. He had to begin considering the lives of others, so that he could minister to them. This had been missing in Jacob's house, but in Egypt, God would teach him. He would see others worse off then himself

This may be where God has you right now. As long as you only think of what God will do for you or for your glory, you'll never accomplish much. God has called us to be part of His great Body in the earth, and when you begin to consider others and their potential, God will enlarge you and move you into a leadership position.

Don't Waste Your Pain on Pity

Those first few days had to be very difficult for Joseph. Was someone there in that caravan used to encourage him? It's not likely. He probably had to encourage himself. This can be very difficult when you feel that you're all alone. It's easy to walk with God when we're with a group of people who are all concentrating on Him, but what about Monday morning, when the realities of life suddenly hit you?

When your moment of need comes, you may not have anyone from whom you can seek wise counsel. You may be all alone in this. It is then that the Word of God, planted in your heart in good times, must sustain you. It will pick you up, encourage you, and send you on your way victorious.

What the brothers did was wrong, and heaven didn't make it right. Yet God was working behind the scenes. And God is working in the background on your behalf too. This account is not just about Joseph. It's a picture of how God is also positioning and preparing you for your purpose.

When you're in a dark place, by yourself and with no one to help you, and God has not answered, *don't waste your pain on pity*. Instead, make up your mind in the midst of the trial what your testimony will be when you come out of the trial—because you will come out of it. You will come out of this trial, and you will come out with a testimony. You need to determine right now what that testimony will be.

> *You will come out of this trial, and you will come out with a testimony.*

We have an old saying: "You can't keep a good man down," and it's true. Life may knock you down, but every time it happens, you have to say to yourself, "I refuse to stay down here." Hold on to God's promise: *"For though a righteous good man falls seven times, he rises again"* (Proverbs 24:16, NIV).

Joseph surely did not want to be in Egypt, and he surely prayed for God to take him back home. But when God didn't intervene in that way, Joseph had a decision to make.

"I can't keep crying myself to sleep every night. Something has to change." That something was him. He had to change.

Stop waiting for God to change your circumstances, and start living for Him in the midst of your circumstances. Realize that God may not change your circumstances, but He can change you. Your purpose is at stake, and, for now at least, this is your place of purpose. Start shining right where you find yourself.

Joseph had to hold on to the dream that he would not always stay where he presently was. He wouldn't always be there. He wasn't sure just why he was in his present situation or how long he would be there, but he decided to do the best he could under the circumstances.

The same holds true for you. Just pass this current test. The sooner you can come to grips with your current situation, the sooner you will be able to move on to the next level.

CHAPTER 9

The Absence of Hope

And Joseph was brought down to Egypt; and Potiphar, an officer of Pharaoh, captain of the guard, an Egyptian, bought him of the hand of the Ishmeelites, which had brought him down thither.

Genesis 39:1

By the time the caravan arrived in Egypt, I can easily imagine Joseph must have finally come to some level of peace with his situation. Realizing that there was no way to escape and return to his father, he most likely had begun to ponder just what the future held for him.

The Slave Market As the Place of Purpose

And then he was in the slave market in Egypt. That must have been very traumatic. But God knew what was best for Joseph, and he didn't allow any of these harsh experiences to be wasted. There can be no doubt that Egypt was the place of Joseph's purpose, and Joseph was just as much in his place of purpose now as he stood in the slave auction as he would be later when he stood in the palace. Although the palace was his ultimate place of purpose, on his journey to the palace he would make several stops.

Each of these stops would, in some way, prepare him for purpose, thus each stop became his present place of purpose. For Joseph, the wrongs that had been done to him were just steppingstones to greater things.

He was sold to an Egyptian with the strange name of Potiphar. In fact, everything about Egypt was strange to Joseph.

A Stranger in a Strange Land

Egypt was a place of a totally different culture and of totally different gods, so Joseph now found himself in a strange place, surrounded by strange people, with a strange culture and customs. He was separated from everything familiar.

Worse, Joseph was a slave, and very quickly he realized what that really meant. We have seen enough slave movies to know of the abuse suffered by slaves, no matter what their nationality. Besides this, Joseph had a total lack of freedom and a total lack of individual rights. He could not choose to do anything. He did what he was told, he did it when he was told to do it, and he did it how he was told to do it. And if he resisted in any way, he no doubt suffered the consequences.

Joseph had no right to argue about anything, to question an order, or even to offer an opinion. He was a prisoner. No longer his own person, he belonged to someone else.

Not understanding the local language also must have presented a great challenge to him. How he overcame this language barrier would probably be a great story in itself. He probably learned Egyptian from the other slaves.

And who were the other slaves in Potiphar's house? Did they befriend Joseph and help him in his new surroundings? Or were they cruel to him? We have no way of knowing. What we do know is that Joseph had much to learn.

Bitter or Better?

Joseph most likely by now was experiencing much anger toward his brothers. They were, after all, the reason for his present state. How would you feel standing among slaves while people looked you over as if you were no more than a prized cattle specimen?

Joseph had to settle some issues with God. "God, You allowed this to happen. You saw everything my brothers did to me, and yet You did absolutely nothing about it. I cried to You in the pit, but You left me there. I cried to You when the Midianites took me, but You did nothing. I cried to You when I was being sold like an animal in the slave auction, but You let me be sold anyway. Now, I don't know where I am or who I'm with, and I don't understand any of it. I thought You loved me. I thought You showed me that You had great purpose for me? What's going on, Lord?"

Did answers come? Maybe, and then maybe not. God wanted Joseph to trust Him, even as He wants us to trust Him during times that we cannot understand His seeming lack of involvement.

At some point, Joseph had a decision to make. He could become bitter, or he could become better. If he had chosen to become bitter, we might never have heard any more from him. His story is different and worth telling because he chose not to become bitter, as most people do.

Joseph's sufferings in Potiphar's house during those early years must have been many, and each time he suffered, he could have blamed it on his brothers. After all, they had taken him from his idyllic life and thrust him into this nightmare existence. No one would have blamed him for doing just that.

Joseph now had to choose whether to allow bitterness and resentment to fester in his soul. He now had to choose whether to dwell on the wrongs done to him and replay them over and over in his mind until hatred consumed him. The choice was his to make: become consumed with bitterness or push everything else aside, let this experience make him a better person, and go on to follow his dream.

Choosing Not to Remember

Personally, I know what it is to fall into bitterness. It's not very hard to do at all. Many years ago, I allowed bitterness to completely consume me. I became disillusioned with life, with people, and eventually with God. In time, this bitterness began to seriously affect my health. I began to experience chest pains.

At first, I didn't take these very seriously, but as they became more frequent, I became alarmed. What was wrong with me? I had numerous visits to the doctors over the next few years. Still, none of them seemed to be able to say why all of this was happening or how this could be alleviated.

Because I was a woman, initially the pains in my chest were not taken very seriously, but when my visits to the doctors became more frequent, even they became concerned.

Doctors are very honest. When they say that they "practice medicine," they're telling the truth. And they did plenty of practicing on me.

I was assigned a cardiologist and given more heart tests than I can now count. I still remember being on the treadmill hooked up to monitors to measure my heart activity during stress tests. I had numerous EKGs and MRIs. The most memorable of these tests was the time they put a huge cable down my throat with some type of camera on the end of it that could look through other tissues and see the heart. They were looking for a hole they felt certain must be there adversely affecting me. They found no hole, and no matter what test they ran, they could find nothing wrong with my heart, and nothing they did seemed to help.

Of course, the doctors were right. There was a problem with my heart, but it was not a physical one. I had allowed the poison of bitterness to affect my heart, and it was causing serious physical and emotional problems. Since the cause of it was not physical, the doctors could not diagnose it. Eventually I came to the conclusion that only Doctor Jesus could change my situation by changing me. And He did.

You may be able to identify with this scenario, for you may know, by experience, how easy it is to become bitter. The problem with bitterness is that although you seem to have every right to become bitter when people do you wrong, all of your bitterness doesn't hurt the other person or persons a bit. Instead, it hurts you.

By the time your health and your personal life are destroyed, the offenders will have gone their way, often without even realizing how they have devastated your life, and you will be left alone to deal with the fallout. Your world may be collapsing around you, and those who were the cause of it seem to have no idea of what you're experiencing or why. They seem to have a serious case of amnesia.

In the midst of my own suffering, God spoke to my heart something that has become a motto for my life to this day. *There are some things I will never forget, but there are some things I choose not to remember.* God graciously gave me the strength to forget the past and the determination not to remember it again in the future.

If you're suffering from memories of the past, I encourage you to put them behind you. Think about it. Why would you allow someone else's past sins to affect your future? God says, *"Vengeance is mine; I will repay"* (Romans 12:19). And He will. He is faithful to His word.

> *Why would you allow someone else's past sins to affect your future?*

The Bible tells us to cast all of our cares on Him for He cares for us (see 1 Peter 5:7). Will you agree to let God handle "them"? I encourage you, wherever you are right now, say this out loud: *There are some things I will never forget, but there are some things I choose not to remember!*

On paper, that sounds like an easy choice, but, of course, it's not quite that easy when we get ready to do it. Sometimes we want to be free of our bitterness, but we just can't seem to stop thinking about what people have done to us. No matter what we do, it's still there.

Stop Ringing the Bell

What can you do when this happens? The story is told of Corrie ten Boom, the well-known Dutch author who chronicled the Christian response to the Nazi occupation of Holland during World War II. She and her father were honored by the people of Israel for their efforts to save Jews from the Nazi death camps. Corrie, her father, and her sister were eventually sent to one of those camps themselves. There, both her father and sister died, and Corrie suffered horrible abuse. Fortunately, her life was spared when the camp was liberated by Allied soldiers.

After being released from the camp, Corrie could not get out of her mind the terrible things that had been done there. These things played and replayed constantly in her mind and made her life miserable. Eventually she took her concerns to a Catholic priest.

"Father," she said, "I have done all that I know to do to forgive these evil men, but dirty spots keep flooding my mind, and I don't know what to do about them."

"Come with me," the priest said, and he led her into the church and then through it and up the steps of the bell tower. Around and around they wound until they reached the level of the great bell. There, standing beside it, the priest said, "I wanted you to see this bell because we're going to ring it in a minute, and I want you to notice what will happen."

They wound their way back down, and the priest took hold of the rope used to ring the bell. "Now, Corrie, he said, "what will happen when I pull this rope?"

"The bell will ring," she said.

"That's right," he answered, and he started pulling the rope. It took a few pulls to get the great bell swinging, but soon it was in full motion, and it began to sound out clearly each time the striker hit the side of the bell.

He let it ring thus for a little while, and then he let go of the rope, looked at Corrie and asked, "What do you hear now, Corrie?"

"It's still ringing," she said. "I can hear it just as before."

"Yes," he agreed. "But let's listen carefully to what happens now." And the two of them stood in silence and anticipation.

For a short while, the bell rang just as before, almost as if the priest was still pulling the rope. Then, slowly, the ringing diminished, as the bell lost motion. It moved slower and slower, each time making less noise, until the two of them were left standing in total silence.

Corrie looked at him in anticipation.

"What do you hear now, child?" the priest asked.

"Nothing, Father," she replied. "The ringing has stopped."

"That's right, Corrie," he said. "Once I stop pulling the rope, the ringing of the bell subsides, and if I don't pull it any more, the sound eventually stops completely. What I'm telling you Corrie is, stop pulling the rope."

That man was very wise. I encourage you to stop rehearsing all the negative words people have said about you and the wrongful actions people have done to you. Whether a best friend, a spouse, a child, a co-worker, a fellow believer, a parent, a boss, a boyfriend or girlfriend … it doesn't matter who did it or what they did. It's not worth losing your soul.

Suffering refines us and makes us shine. A diamond is a diamond only because it has undergone great pressure for long periods of time. Before that, it was just a piece of dirty coal.

Would you adorn your finger with a piece of coal? Not really. But after it has undergone severe pressure, it takes on an entirely different appearance. It's not dull any more, it's not dirty anymore, and now everyone recognizes it as a precious gem of great value.

A diamond shines, and you can shine too if you make a decision to withstand the pressures of life. Keep a smile on your face—no matter what is happening around you, God is polishing you, and He will continue this process if you will allow Him to.

If, on the other hand, you refuse to forgive, you'll become a miserable person, and you'll make everyone around you miserable. You can't afford to let that happen. So don't allow any unforgiveness to remain in your heart.

Pain is Inevitable, but Misery is Optional

Let me take a moment to tell you about my deliverance from bitterness. My husband often makes the statement "Pain is inevitable, but misery is optional." When I first heard him say that, I had just been delivered from my state of bitterness, and I thought, "You know, it's true. Pain is inevitable, and misery is optional, but that's the second time around." Let me explain.

I have said several times already in this book that if you keep on living, sooner or later life will bring you pain. That's not a great revelation. But we do not always choose to go to the place of misery. Sometimes we get lost and unexpectedly find ourselves there.

Have you ever been on the freeway, driving to some destination, and accidentally gotten off on the wrong exit? When you tried to get back on the freeway, you realized that you didn't know where the entrance was. You drove around a little, trying to find the entrance, only to find yourself in some strange neighborhood. You stopped and asked directions, but the person you asked either began scratching their head (a sure sign that they didn't know themselves), or they couldn't speak good English.

This happened to me a few years ago when I was with some friends. Following the directions we had been given took us several miles out of our way, and we found ourselves driving in the dark—not knowing where we were going, but sure that we were going the wrong way.

That's how misery works. The first time you go there, you don't realize where you're going. Then, when you suddenly find yourself in that miserable state, you don't know how to get out of it. Your heart plays tricks on you, and your mind refuses to let go. When you eventually get back on track and recognize all the trauma you went through during the experience, it is then that you determine you'll never make that same mistake again. So misery is optional the second time.

I Will Not Praise You!

Allow me the privilege of giving you some directions without scratching my head. During my season of bitterness, I had an experience that not only delivered me from this state, but also gave me a message for the masses.

I was in church one day and our choir was singing under a powerful anointing from God. Our church people are very lively and expressive. That day they were responding to God with such joy that they were, as we say, "swinging from the chandeliers" (not literally, of course).

Our praise team was singing with the choir, and the praise leader exhorted the audience to "wave your hands and praise the Lord." But that particular day, I was not about to praise God for anything. I didn't understand where He was, and why He was allowing such trials in my life. So I looked up to heaven and told God, "I will not praise You. Where are You? How could You leave me like this?"

To make my point more forceful, I balled up my fist and, once again, said with fierce determination, "I will not praise You!"

The Absence of Hope

While I was saying all of this, tears were streaming down my face. I was not crying audibly. I was hurt, but only tears came that day. My days of loud crying were behind me, and some of you know exactly what I'm speaking of here. There are times in life when we have no more eruptions of anger or occurrences of tears. Outbursts of these emotions mean that we can still feel, we're still hopeful, and thus, we still care. When hope is not fulfilled, tears are less frequent.

When hope remains unfulfilled for a long time, it eventually leaves, and when there is an absence of hope, this is truly dangerous. The reason this is such a dangerous state is that it usually marks the fact that you have fallen into bitterness, or you're swiftly approaching it. This is where suicide, murder, and even insanity get their hold on people.

The Place of No Return

A very close friend of mine told me of a time when the problems in her marriage left her in a state of despair. She had gone through many years of abuse at the hands of her insanely jealous husband. He insisted that she go to work dressed very plainly, with her hair braided like a small girl and wearing no makeup. They argued violently on a regular basis, and she was constantly belittled in front of her children. This was a serious case of psychological abuse.

One day, after one of these episodes, she sat in her dining room pondering her life. She was alone and miserable. No one could help her. It seemed that she was destined to go on this way for the rest of her life.

She sat there for a while, as if in a trance, and when she looked up, she saw a door. A voice beckoned her to walk through the door, telling her that on the other side of it was peace. The voice kept calling, "Come! Just walk through the door." And she rose to obey.

Just as she was about to walk through the door, she heard another voice, this one with a fearsome warning: "If you walk through that door, you'll never come back."

She had a choice to make. These two voices were opposing voices. Which one was God's? She was able to shake off the trance-like state into which she had fallen, and prayed for God to guide her. Later, she called me to tell me about this strange experience. She was convinced that the door being shown to her was the door to insanity.

What does your problem have to do with [God's] majesty?

I praise God to this day that my friend did not go through that door. Because of her experience, I have often wondered how many people are in insane asylums today because they made a choice to go there, not realizing what was behind the door and that it was a place of no return.

Praise Him through the Tears

As I stood in church that Sunday morning in pain, refusing to praise God, He looked beyond my fault and saw my need, as the popular hymn states so eloquently. He knows just what we need and when we need it. That day, God knew that I needed to hear from Him, and that's exactly what took place.

I haven't had the privilege of hearing God audibly many times in my life. Most of the time, He speaks to me through an inner word, but that day I heard His voice audibly. He said two things that changed my life forever, and I pray they will change yours too. He said, "Charlyn, *What does your problem have to do with My majesty? And what does your pain have to do with My glory?* You don't praise Me because of what I do for you; you praise Me because of Who I am!" Those words ministered so deeply to me that I lifted up my hands and began to praise God. To this day, I'm still praising him.

Nothing had changed in my life. All of the circumstances, situations and people were still there. But on that day, I learned what it meant to praise God through my tears.

Hallelujah Anyhow!

The wonderful thing about that situation was this: I determined that I would never go to the place of bitterness or misery again. I learned how to hold on to God, even when I didn't see Him, and I learned to say, "Hallelujah anyhow!"

That event took place almost twenty years ago, and since then each time I have gone through the valley of the shadow of death, the words *hallelujah anyhow* have encouraged, sustained, upheld, and ministered to me. They have been my lifeline to Jesus and helped me to keep every trial in perspective.

In times of joy, we often say, "Hallelujah!" That's because everything's going well, and we want to thank God for it. But during our times of despair and disappointment, we need to learn to say, "Hallelujah anyhow!"

"My situation might be bleak, but hallelujah anyhow!"

"There's too much month at the end of the money, but hallelujah anyhow!"

"My spouse might be acting crazy, but hallelujah anyhow!"

"My children are acting like heathens, but hallelujah anyhow!"

"My boss appears to be Satan reincarnated, but hallelujah anyhow!"

"Hallelujah anyhow! Hallelujah anyhow! Hallelujah anyhow!"

God gives us lessons to pass on to others, and it's been my privilege to encourage thousands with this one. I guarantee that if you, too, will learn these two words, your life too will be better, you'll have more peace, and your joy will return.

You can begin practicing this today. In fact, let me encourage you to say this out loud right now: "Hallelujah anyhow!"

The politician Jesse Jackson is often quoted as saying "Keep hope alive." That is my prayer for you, as you read this book. I pray that from this day forth, you will never again experience the absence of hope, but will keep hope alive in your heart and soul.

CHAPTER 10

Preparing For Purpose

The details of Joseph's ordeal in Egypt are not recorded because they're unimportant. Whatever he suffered is not worthy of mention. What is important is that, at some point, he began turning things around, and he did that by maintaining a good spirit and working hard at what had become his lot in life for the moment.

It was at this point that the Scriptures record an amazing encouragement:

And the Lord was with Joseph, and he was a prosperous man; and he was in the house of his master the Egyptian. And his master saw that the Lord was with him, and that the Lord made all that he did to prosper in his hand.

Genesis 39:2-3

Under even these dire circumstances, *"the Lord was with him,"* and *"the LORD made all that he did to prosper in his hand."* Wow! That's powerful!

Joseph had been stripped of his wonderful coat of many colors, but he had not been stripped of the favor of God. The favor followed Joseph because God was with him. Even in that strange and lonely place, he still experienced the presence of God.

This favor was now evident to all those who worked with him in Egypt. Just as God had blessed him in Canaan, Joseph was still being blessed in Egypt.

The text goes on to report more details of his amazing blessing:

And Joseph found grace in his [Potiphar's] sight, and he served him: and he made him overseer over his house, and all that he had he put into his hand. And it came to pass from the time that he had made him overseer in his house, and over all that he had, that the Lord blessed the Egyptian's house for Joseph's sake; and the blessing of the Lord was upon all that he had in the house, and in the field. And he left all that he had in Joseph's hand; and he knew not ought he had, save the bread which he did eat.

Genesis 39:4-6

What is not immediately apparent is that some time had elapsed between verse 1, which records the fact that Potiphar bought Joseph as a slave in Egypt, and verses 2 and 3 that speak of Joseph's prosperity in Potiphar's house and verses 4 through 6 that speak of his elevation to the post of majordomo, or overseer, over all that Potiphar possessed. This did not all happen overnight. It happened over a period of years. As Joseph matured, maintained his dream, and persisted against every obstacle, the Lord demonstrated favor upon his life.

When you feel all alone, know that you're not really alone at all. The Lord is with you. He is Jehovah-Shammah, the Lord ever-present. The fact that He was with Joseph changed everything, and His presence in your life will also make all the difference.

As we can see, people around Joseph got blessed, and that should be true in our lives as well. Because God is with us, if others get close to us, His blessings should rub off on others. I expect the people I'm around to be blessed just because they're around me, and just because God is with me.

This is a scriptural promise. If you love God, then expect your household to be blessed. If you have an unsaved spouse or work for a secular company, for example, expect some of the favor God has put upon you to rub off on them.

The Secret of Promotion

Of course, Joseph didn't start working the first day as the majordomo for the estate of Potiphar. He started out as the lowliest of slaves, but the fact that he chose to focus on God caused him to excel at everything he did. Because of this, he quickly rose in the ranks, until he was over absolutely everything in Potiphar's house.

We, too, must look upon every test that comes our way as an opportunity for advancement. When we have proven ourselves faithful, we, like Joseph, will be promoted. It's guaranteed.

Joseph had resolved in his mind that God had not abandoned him, that God had permitted this current situation for some reason, and that he would be better off for having experienced it. Then, once he began to set his hands to things, he did them well. He was a faithful servant, and God honored him in every way.

Potiphar was not a believer in Jehovah. He was a heathen man, and yet he noticed the favor that was upon Joseph's life. The Egyptians didn't believe in the true God, and that was one of the reasons God had sent Joseph to Egypt. But as heathen as these Egyptians were, they recognized that God's hand was upon Joseph.

What about you? Do the people around you recognize that favor is upon you? Whether heathen or Christian, do they see that you're different? Is your life making a difference in those with whom you come in contact?

Joseph learned many things while being over Potiphar's house. He learned farming, the care of livestock, and fisheries. He learned how to manage money properly and how to keep books and account for monies spent. He learned personnel management. And, as he learned, he was preparing for his ultimate purpose. He hadn't gotten to know any of these things in his father's house, because there he was the privileged son. As a slave, he was required to learn them.

We cannot say exactly when and how Joseph caught his master's attention. What is sure is that he received one promotion after another under one supervisor and then another and another until eventually Potiphar himself recognized that Joseph's God was the source of the prosperity he was experiencing. Though the particulars of this season in Joseph's life occupy only a few verses in the Bible, these verses represent years of hard work and faithful service, many tears, and many victories. Joseph had learned the secret of promotion.

Still, life could not have been easy for Joseph. As a man of destiny, he was a constant target for the enemy, who is always seeking to block God's purpose for our lives. But because Joseph chose to remain faithful to God, Satan could do nothing to deter him. Instead, the young man kept moving up the ladder of success.

A New Test

Now that Joseph had been able to overcome his circumstances and rise to prosperity, a new temptation arose. This temptation was very subtle and very dangerous:

> *And Joseph was a goodly person, and well favoured. And it came to pass after these things, that his master's wife cast her eyes upon Joseph; and she said, Lie with me.*

> Genesis 39:6-7

Besides catching Potiphar's eye, Joseph also caught the eye of Mrs. Potiphar. The Bible makes it very clear that Joseph was unusually good looking, what women today refer to as "fine." In this respect, he must have taken after his mother. By this time, he was most likely in his early twenties.

The hard work of Potiphar's house had served Joseph well, and now his body (over which the Egyptians were not known to wear a lot of clothes) was well "buffed." Joseph truly seemed to have been a tall, dark, and handsome figure. No wonder he began to catch the eye of Potiphar's wife!

This was a very difficult thing for Joseph. If his master's wife wanted anything, who was he to resist her?

It is very possible that this woman had done similar things with other slave men. After all, Potiphar was a very busy man, and his wife must have been attractive enough in her own right. The captain of Pharaoh's guard would not have had an ugly wife. Whatever the case, now her attention was turned on Joseph, and she began to make very brazen advances toward him.

And what was Joseph feeling about all of this? Well, try to put yourself in his place for a moment.

This young man was far from home and very lonely. His mother was dead, and he had not seen his father or brothers for many years. He was a growing young man, at or around the age when scientists have discovered men are at their sexual peak, and therefore his hormones were raging. He had never been with a woman, and we have no reason to believe that he would be anything but normal in regard to physical desires.

In one sense of the word, how could he refuse this women? After all, she was the mistress of the house, and he was her slave. Plus, if anyone could ever justify sexual immorality, it would have been Joseph. Giving in to the demands of this woman might actually make his life easier, for she had the power to show him great favor.

If he gave in to her, he would no longer have to work around the house. He could enjoy a life of leisure, entertaining the mistress of the house through the long days while her husband was away. Oh, there are a lot of Potiphar's wives in this world today, and far too often, I'm afraid, they get their way.

Being found attractive to a woman of this stature could not have been an unpleasant feeling for Joseph. Most people have a tendency to enjoy attention. Such attention may come to them for a variety of reasons, ranging from physical attributes to their mental capacities. If the attention is not "pure," they may choose to ignore it. But that doesn't lessen the fact that someone has found them appealing.

Because of her position in Egyptian society, Mrs. Potiphar would surely want to be discreet about any affair they might have. So who would know? Given all of the circumstances, what did Joseph have to lose?

This may all sound like logical thinking, but Joseph thought otherwise. He did resist, deciding that he could not sin against his master, Potiphar, and he could not sin against his God.

A Fatal Attraction

This is a wonderful place to give a warning to men. If you're being tempted to have an illicit affair with a woman, and she promises you that she won't tell, don't believe her. She will. She may not think she will, but eventually, she will. You can take it to the bank.

First, if you're married and her heart becomes attached to you, more often than not, she'll start to envision herself as your wife, and then she'll want the privileges of that position. Eventually, she'll resent the time you spend with your wife at home, to the point that she'll be angered by you having sexual relations with your own wife. Your wife has now become her enemy. It's your wife who's keeping the two of you from your "life" together.

You'll want to protect your wife from this mistake you'll soon see you've made, and that becomes your "girlfriend's" weapon. Her threat of telling your wife about the relationship is now something to be used to keep you in line.

Now, if you really hit the jackpot, you could end up with a total wacko. All you saw was her wonderful body and her sexy appealing words. But now she may be threatening your family with harm. In her mind, she feels that if she can't have you, no one will.

Or you may have gotten involved with Wacko's sister. She's the woman who threatens the man with suicide. "I'll kill myself if you leave," she tells you. She uses this many times to make you afraid to break off the relationship; she really has no intention of killing herself. But you don't know that, and you feel trapped. After all, you already made one terrible mistake, and you don't want her death on your conscience.

This woman may just be unstable enough to actually carry through with her threat. You simply don't know if she will take her life, or if she's just threatening you with this.

Whatever the case, you're now living in hell, and you don't know how to get out. If you've never seen the movie *Fatal Attraction* with Michael Douglas, you may want to go rent it. It may help you.

Even if the relationship doesn't end up so ugly, if nothing else, this woman will, most likely, tell her friends, especially her best friend. They will talk on the phone about you. On night's when you're at home where you should be, the woman who, in some bizarre way, now thinks she's supposed to be true to you, will converse with her friends and tell them why she's staying at home, and is no longer interested in other men. When the two of you have a disagreement, she'll need someone to talk to. Usually, she'll tell her best friend, and then her best friend will tell her best friend and so on.

Finally, in today's technological age, there are no secrets. All cell phone conversations are now recorded by someone. A cell phone is nothing short of a two-way transmitter. This is the reason you often begin hearing someone's unknown voice in the midst of your cell-phone conversations.

Think about that. How in the world did we all hear conversations between Scott Peterson and Amber Fry on the evening news? (This was the man in Southern California accused of killing his wife, Lacy and unborn son, Conner.) I'm sure that Scott Peterson never dreamed that their conversations would one day come back to haunt them.

And that could be you. The Bible tells us that what is done in darkness will come to light (see Luke 12:3). It also gives an admonition to men in the book of Proverbs:

Drink water from your own cistern, and running water from your own well....

Rejoice with the wife of your youth. as a loving deer and a graceful doe, let her breasts satisfy you at all times.

Proverbs 5:15 and 18-19, NKJ

Why are men encouraged to do this? Because when it comes to unfaithfulness in marriage with another woman, the Bible shows:

For she has cast down many wounded. And all who were slain by her were strong men. Her house is the way to hell, descending to the chambers of death.

Proverbs 7:26-27, NKJ

We can also learn from the mistakes of others. Television, whether the fiction of movies or the truth of the evening news, is full of stories such as these. I encourage you stay at home, men, and learn to love your wife. If you feel nothing for her, ask God to change that, and He will. He said, *"Ask, and you will receive"* (John 16:23, NKJ).

God is the God of answered prayer. Ask Him to give you a brand new love for your wife. Stop focusing on her negative points, and look in the mirror. Ask God to make you the wonderful husband He wants you to be. Finally, take all the wonderful things you have been saying or doing, or thinking about saying or doing for the other woman, and transfer all that attention and money onto your wife. After all, your peace, and more importantly, your purpose is at stake. You don't want to risk it on temporal pleasure and end up with long-lasting sorrow.

The argument that no one will ever know seems to fool many. It may well seem rational at the moment, but in the end, everyone will know. When I was a small girl, I remember hearing my mother say, "Someone sees everything." She was right. And though that "someone" may only be God, if that is the case, He's enough. Joseph believed this too, and it saved the day for him:

But he refused, and said unto his master's wife, Behold, my master wotteth not what is with me in the house, and he hath committed all that he hath to my hand; There is none greater in this house than I; neither hath he kept back any thing from me but thee, because thou art his wife: how then can I do this great wickedness, and sin against God?

Genesis 39:8-9

That was a praiseworthy answer, but it was, by no means, the end of the matter. The fact that Joseph resisted only seemed to make the woman bolder and more demanding. The challenge of the chase seemed to appeal all the more to Mrs. Potiphar. Every day now she approached him suggestively, using wiles that we can only imagine, wearing what we can only imagine, in an effort to change his mind:

And it came to pass ... [that] she spake to Joseph day by day ... to lie by her, or to be with her.

Genesis 39:10

I picture the woman actually rubbing up against Joseph, and if she did this *"day by day,"* how could Joseph continue to resist? She had him over a barrel so to speak (or so she thought), and she kept stepping up the pace of her bold and brazen approach to him.

"Joseph," the woman must have been urging, "I know you have to miss your family. It must be terrible to be so far from home. I can make you forget all of your pain. You're such a good person, and you deserve to be happy like anyone else. Come on, Joseph. Put down those things, and let's go to my room and have some fun. You're off duty for the rest of the day."

Joseph was wise. When he saw this woman coming, he moved on to another room, trying his best to avoid her. It had become obvious to him what was on her mind, long before she became so blatant about it. And he had to keep several paces ahead of her.

Each day we must make it a goal to seek God....

To a young man in Joseph's situation, this must have seemed awfully tempting, almost demanding, and somewhat irresistible. At home, he might have been married by now, but as a slave in this strange land, he had no wife to share his life with and no prospect of having one any time soon. Still, Joseph continued to resist.

Satan Never Gives Up

Even as Joseph was tempted day by day, our enemy, Satan, comes after us time after time to tempt us to go against the Word and will of God. If we win today, he formulates a new plan for tomorrow. He's like the Ever-Ready Bunny, and like a Timex watch, he "takes a licking and keeps on ticking."

This is why the Word of God tells us that *the inward man is renewed day by day*" (2 Corinthians 4:16). Each day we must make it a goal to seek God, even to the point of telling Him over and over again:

Thank You for another day, Lord. How can I honor You with my life today? What is Your will for my life today? Lord, open my eyes and show me the traps the enemy has planned for me this day. Today is Your day in my life, Lord.

He harkened not unto her.

Genesis 39:10

This was phenomenal! Joseph was not about to sin against his master and put in jeopardy all of the progress he had made by God's grace, and he was not about to sin against God and lose the favor that had made him what he was. He knew what sin was, and he wanted no part of it.

Of course, this didn't mean that the woman would give up. Far from it. She was very persistent and began to think of ways to trap Joseph. In time, she hit upon a plan that she was sure would work.

One day she made sure that none of the other servants were in the house. With them out of the way, she once again tried to seduce Joseph. As before, he refused her advances. But Mrs. Potiphar had made up her mind, and her flesh was raging with desire. This time she was going to get what she wanted. With everyone gone, she no longer needed to be subtle. When Joseph refused her, she physically took hold of him and actually tried to force herself upon him:

And it came to pass about this time, that Joseph went into the house to do his business; and there was none of the men of the house there within. And she caught him by his garment, saying, Lie with me.

Genesis 39:11-12

This was not an invitation; it was a command. And it was a command from a person of authority to a slave who had learned always to obey or suffer the consequences. But even though Joseph had learned his lesson well, this time was different. He could not obey this woman, for if he did, he would be dishonoring higher authorities: Potiphar, for one, and more importantly, God Himself.

Joseph had been faithful until now. Could he remain faithful through this severe test? So, although the two of them were all alone in the house, when she reached for him, Joseph did the wisest thing he could possibly have done in that moment. He turned and ran as fast as he could. And I, for one, say, good for Joseph! Oh, that we had more Josephs today!

Run, Forest, Run

One of the things I, along with so many others, was amused with in the movie *Forest Gump* was the fact that he ran his way through life to fame. And I always think about Forest Gump running from danger, when I think about Joseph. In the case of Forest Gump, his Jenny's words were expressions of wisdom to all: "Run, Forest, run!"

He left his garment in her hand, and fled, and got him out.

Genesis 39:12

What a wonderful lesson Joseph presents. Though he was alone and lonely, uncommitted, and at the height of his sexual prowess, when this desirable woman promised him some sort of escape from reality, he did not think it a good enough excuse to sin.

Although there is never an excuse for sin, how many times have we heard someone say:

"I felt so alone, and I needed someone."

"We just started talking, and then one thing led to another."

"Before I knew what was happening, we were going further, and 'somehow' I got myself into this mess."

I think the best one I've heard was, "We're just friends." It's strange how being "just friends" has a way of getting out of hand very quickly!

Let's explore these excuses for a moment. What are people thinking when they fall so foolishly? For example, why would someone who is single and living alone have a man (or a woman) whom they are attracted to in their apartment at one o'clock in the morning? They begin heavy kissing and heavy caressing, and then they're surprised when things "somehow" get out of hand and go too far. What in the world did they expect to happen?

A word to the wise: just because you think you're in love and hope that one day the two of you will get married, that doesn't make it right, and nor does it mean it will happen that way. Even if you do end up marrying each other, you won't be able to trust each other. After all, if you couldn't contain yourself with her (or him) now, what makes you think they'll trust you to contain yourself with others in the future? *"He who has an ear, let him hear"* (Revelation 2:29, 3:6 and 13:9, NIV).

A Man Must Know His Limitations

Joseph was wiser than that. As Clint Eastwood said in his movie "Magnum Force," "A man's got to know his limitations." Joseph knew his, and so he knew just what he had to do.

Many people would have at least flirted with sin. Joseph took a stand and refused to do this, for flirting with sin is always a bad mistake.

Joseph also did not stay there trying to reason with the woman or enjoying her attentions for even a few minutes. He seemed to realize how truly dangerous this situation was to his spiritual health. So he did the best thing; he ran.

He didn't walk fast. He didn't bother to say, "Please excuse me." He didn't stop to try to retrieve his coat. He was gone, and that was all there was to it. He ran from the house as fast as he could, and the woman was left holding the garment.

And what will you do when it happens to you? Sin will inevitably come knocking on your door. It may not be the same sin that Joseph faced, but it will be sin nevertheless. Something might tempt one person and not tempt another. Your particular temptation might involve your temper, your tongue, your flesh, or your pride. Your temptation might be in the realm of finances or something else entirely. Whatever the case, determine in your heart now that when temptation comes knocking, you will ask Jesus to please answer the door. And you will refuse to allow your heart or mind to carry you away. Always remember that you have the power within you to just say no!

You can strive to be like Jesus, when He said:

The prince of this world cometh, and hath nothing in me.

John 14:30

In other words, when Satan came looking for a way, any way, to pull Jesus away from the Father, he found nothing to hook onto. Satan is also looking for just the right time and place to attack you. Even now, he's looking for that hook in your life, that one thing he can grab onto and pull you away from your convictions and from your God. Don't lose your testimony. Don't break God's heart and bring shame to His kingdom. Cling to God and ask for His help in moments of temptation.

Jesus came to this earth for a purpose, and giving in to Satan would have disqualified Him from that purpose. He needed to be tempted and yet remain without sin to be qualified to die in our place, and so that His death would be an acceptable sacrifice to God.

In the same way, God has placed you on this earth for a purpose. You may not be here for all of mankind, as Jesus was, but you're here to touch some of mankind. In Chapter 1, we talked about purpose being "a terrible thing to waste." What is just as tragic is when purpose is lost, or, I should say, when purpose is thrown away. Don't throw away your purpose. Guard it with all your heart.

A Desperate Housewife

I believe I'm safe in saying that Potiphar's wife had no intention of leaving Potiphar and marrying Joseph. After all, Potiphar was rich, and Joseph was still just a slave. She just wanted to be entertained. She just wanted to have some fun. Then Joseph could go back to his quarters, and she would get on with her life.

Ms. Potiphar is like modern women today who go after the wrong men. They do it, not for love, but for position. The fact that Joseph had risen to such a height of respect intrigued her. And, she was tired of Potiphar. Perhaps he seemed to be always preoccupied with his financial matters, or with his duties in the empire, or, perhaps, with his own little secret social life. We're not told why she had no problem violating her marriage vows, but she seems to have been like the women on a currently popular television program called "Desperate Housewives." The fact that this program is now the highest rated show on television is a sad commentary on American life.

The fact that Joseph was so young and yet in such a position of authority may have been what caused Potiphar's wife to have such a desire for him. That's not to say that she fell in love with him. Just the opposite. She only wanted his body. But why was she particularly drawn to Joseph?

There is something about a man in a position of power that attracts women. Men need to be aware of this, especially men in the ministry. Deacons, elders, pastors, teachers, administrators, you're all targets for lustful women, women on assignment from hell.

If you find yourself in this position, ask yourself, "Does this woman who is making advances at me, really like me as a person?" Maybe. And then maybe not. She is probably attracted more to your position, and she wants to be identified with you because of it. Her attraction may have nothing to do with you as a person.

Joseph was a challenge for Mrs. Potiphar, and she was sure that she could eventually break down his resistance. When she couldn't, she was humiliated and furious beyond words. Although Joseph had taken a stand for right, that stand would now cost him, and cost him dearly.

CHAPTER 11

The Price of Purpose

The whole "Mrs. Potiphar experience" must have been very painful for Joseph. The atmosphere was so emotionally charged, and he sensed that nothing good could come of it—no matter what choice he made. If he accepted the woman's advances, he would experience the immediate loss of favor with God and the inevitable loss of favor with Potiphar. If he didn't, he would experience the wrath of Mrs. Potiphar herself.

Hell Hath No Fury Like a Woman Scorned

It was an impossible situation, but Joseph decided to side with God. After all, God had been faithful to him when he was in the pit, on the slave block, and in Potiphar's house. He was there in Potiphar's house because God had continued his kindness and brought him there. Despite this new development, Joseph knew that he had to hold on to God.

But taking a stand against sin always costs us something. In taking a stand, Joseph was pitting himself against his master's wife. That was a dangerous move. Most of us are familiar with the old saying, "Hell hath no fury like a woman scorned." This story proves the validity of that statement.

Joseph refused Mrs. Potiphar's advances, and now he had a scorned woman on his hands. How dare this slave treat her with such contempt! How dare he reject her as if she were some undesirable? *"He"* did not want *"her"*? This caused her to seethe with anger and burn with rage. As far as she was concerned, Joseph's rejection was a challenge to her authority.

Underneath the anger, Mrs. Potiphar also felt humiliated and shamed by Joseph's rejection, as any woman would. His rejection had quickly thrown water on the flaming passions of the flesh she'd been feeling for such a long time. Now extinguished, those passions took on a new form—a deadly obsessive and vengeful anger. She would get her revenge. She would show this defiant slave who was boss. She would teach him a lesson!

And the Academy Award for Best Actress Goes to...

She lost no time in taking revenge upon him. She concocted a story, brought her anger under control, and put on an Oscar-worthy performance. She called all the men of the household in and told them that Joseph had tried to molest her, and had fled only when she cried out for help. She then held up her prized piece of evidence; the coat he had left as he had fled from the scene of the crime.

When her husband came home, she repeated the now well-rehearsed story to him, and he believed her ... at least at the first.

Potiphar was understandably angry. He had trusted Joseph, and now this? He was so angry that he took Joseph, until then a very valuable commodity in his household, and had him imprisoned immediately.

As he did so, Potiphar must have wondered what had possessed him to buy the Hebrew slave in the first place. He should have known better. What did he need with such a young and obviously green foreigner? He had endured his lack of culture, his lack of language, and his lack of work experience, and had pushed him up the ladder of success—only to be treated in this despicable way. Well, he had learned his lesson, and he would never trust another Hebrew.

We can only imagine what he said to the jailers. He probably wanted Joseph to suffer before he was put to death. And, because of this, I cannot help but think that Joseph was mistreated in jail. After all, Potiphar was a mighty figure in the kingdom. Joseph, a foreign slave had brought shame to the first lady of the house. Even in today's society, there are different levels of inmates.

Joseph was imprisoned as an attempted rapist. I would lay odds on the fact that the prison guards felt justified in beating this foreigner and beating him badly.

The Testimony You Leave Behind

For Joseph's part, as he was led away in chains from Potiphar's house that day, he had no chance to tell anyone, his fellow servants or other members of the household who had come to know him well, that he was innocent of the charges. All the years he had been a testimony to his God had now ended with this. What would they think of him? What would they think about his God? He could only hope that they knew him better than to believe the lie that had been told. But whatever they believed, there was nothing he could do about it now.

Taking a stand for God in this crazy world of ours sometimes carries with it unexpected consequences. Like Joseph, you might get fired for doing the right thing, you might lose a friend, or you might suffer economic consequences. Whatever the cost, it's always right and proper to take a stand for the Lord—on your job, in your home, in your community, and in the world at large.

When you take a stand for holiness, and suffer the injustice of people gossiping and telling all kinds of lies about you, all you can do is hope that your testimony has been such that those who were in your presence come to the conclusion that the accusations against you could, in no way, be true. They just don't sound like the person they know, and, so, as far as they're concerned, you're innocent until proven guilty.

You should also be prepared for people you thought were your friends to believe the worst about you. It will happen. Hopefully, when bad things are said about you, people will know you well enough to say, "I can't believe that because I've known them now for so long, and they're just not like that." But history proves this is not always the case.

That's Really None of Your Business

My husband is senior pastor of one of the largest churches in Southern California, Loveland Church. As the pastor and pastor's wife of such a prominent ministry, he and I have had more than our share of lies told about us. We take this in stride. After all, it's Satan's job to do all that he can to discredit the saints. The more effective you are in the Kingdom, the more intense his attacks will be.

On one of those occasions, many years ago, when we built our house, the rumors became so cruel that I remember saying to myself, "If I didn't know me and heard these evil lies, I would think that I was a terrible person."

I've learned that it's not worth it to try to track a rumor back to its source.

I've learned that it's not worth it to try to track a rumor back to its source. It's next to impossible to try to get to the root of it. All you usually end up with is wasted time. This is because most people who spread gossip don't want their name attached to the gossip. Because of this mindset, when someone attempts to tell me any negative information about another, I ask them three things: (1) What is their purpose in sharing the information with me? Is there something I can do about it? (2) Have they talked to the person involved about the information they're sharing? (3) Most importantly, can I attach their name to information they're sharing?

I don't accept the excuse: "I want you to pray about it." Ninety-nine percent of the time they have not prayed about it themselves, and they're just using this to excuse their actions. Anyway, those three questions will stop gossips dead in their tracks.

As for you, you need to know you're not a trash receptacle, and you shouldn't want garbage festering in your heart. For my part, if the information doesn't concern me as a person, and I'm not being asked to intervene as a minister, then it is none of my business. If you don't meet that same criteria, then it's none of your business either.

Although I don't try to track down the source of rumors spread against me, I do try to live a life that will make those who have been in my presence greatly question them. That's all I can do, and that's all you can do too. God is Jehovah Saboeth; the captain of the armies of heaven. It's His responsibility to defend me, so I leave those who come against me with their mouth for God to fight.

And, in this case, God fought for me. Some months after the rumors had run their course, I ran into a woman who had initially believed them. She told me, "After I thought about it, I told my mother and my sister, 'What is being said about her simply doesn't line up with what I've seen in her.' " What a blessing! But the great lesson in this: this woman was not particularly fond of me, and that was the reason that she had been so quick to believe the worst. Still, even she could not hold on to the lies for long.

The testimony Joseph had left behind was all that he had now. It alone had to speak for him, as he was powerless to speak for himself.

Favor had followed Joseph all the way from the land of Canaan to Egypt and Potiphar's house. Would that prove to be the case now that he was about to become a common criminal doing a long stint in prison?

Go to Jail! Go Directly to Jail! Do Not Pass Go! Do Not Collect $200!

And Joseph's master took him, and put him into the prison, a place where the king's prisoners were bound: and he was there in the prison.

Genesis 39:20

What a terrible turn of events! Joseph had done nothing to deserve prison and its abuse. In fact, he had done everything exactly as he should have. His conduct was exemplary. Even though it would have been very easy for him to sin, he had refused. And now this! It was all so unfair!

On top of it all, it was Potiphar, the man Joseph had caused to prosper, the man he had served faithfully, and the man he had refused to take advantage of and sin against, who had believed the worst of him and had placed him in prison. Whatever happened to justice? At that moment, the world seemed like a very unfair place.

Right Is Often Rewarded with Wrong

We should not be surprised at what happened to Joseph. It's nothing unusual that a man or woman should suffer for taking a stand for God. It happens. When you insist on doing things God's way, you rile up the spirits that control this world, and they often lash out against you. Just because you have taken a stand for God will not necessarily mean that you will be rewarded. No one may pat you on the back. Instead, people will often talk about you and against you and worse.

It's not unusual for good people to suffer through no fault of their own. It happens in a variety of situations. For instance, good people are sometimes overlooked by their friends, by their employers, or even by their own family members. Sometimes good people are abandoned by a mate, even though they have been a faithful spouse. There is no explanation. It just happens. It's not fair, but people have a free will, and you cannot force people to treat you as they should.

Many families conduct regular family reunions. While attending these, you may not feel comfortable doing the things some of your family members do—even if you used to participate in them. You were not a Christian then, but now you have changed and want to maintain a good testimony. You now want to be to them an example of holy living in the hope that your family members will want to accept Jesus for themselves. Therefore, you now cannot participate in the drinking and trash talking that often accompany events like these. And when you don't, you will suddenly become an outsider. The same is true of many class reunions.

"Hey, how are you? It's so good to see you. Come on, have a drink with me."

"Thank you, but I don't drink."

"Oh, really? You're better than us now? When did you become such a Goody-Two-Shoes? You used to be just like the rest of us." And from that moment on, you may struggle to be a part of things and find that you cannot.

You might try explaining to your former classmates that you are what you are by the grace of God, but often they don't want to hear it, or they may be too drunk to pay much attention to what you're saying.

As he sat in the prison in Egypt, no doubt Joseph wondered many times if he would have been better off to have given in to the demands of Potiphar's wife. After all, what had his stand for purity gotten him? If he had given in to her, he might still be over Potiphar's house, and he could have enjoyed the comfort of the relationship with the woman—however short-lived.

Why do we sometimes suffer for going the extra mile and for living a pure and undefiled life? The reasons are not always clear to us at the time, but God has a purpose in all that He does. And you will be a better person for having gone through these periods of temptation, no matter who the enemy uses to bring them.

As Paul wrote:

What shall we then say to these things? If God be for us, who can be against us?

Romans 8:31

No, Joseph was not sorry that he had done the right thing, and you must not be sorry either.

Three Steps Forward and Five Back

And where was God in all of this? Why would He allow a pagan woman to cause His servant Joseph to suffer so? Why had fire not fallen from heaven to consume her?

Joseph had already suffered indignities at the hands of his brothers who hated him, he had suffered indignities at the hands of the Ishmaelites, to whom he was nothing more than some property to be sold or traded, he had suffered indignities in the slave market, he had suffered indignities at the hands of Potiphar's wife, and now here he was in prison to suffer even more indignities. Why was God permitting all of this?

None of this had been part of his dream. Would it ever come to pass? And what would happen to him now? Was all lost?

He had struggled back from the blackness of the pit, struggled back again from the terrible trip to Egypt, and then struggled back again from the slave auction and from the humiliation of having to serve in Potiphar's house. And he had done it all so well that he had found favor in the sight of his master, an important man in Egypt. The result was that he had risen quickly up the ranks and actually taken charge of everything.

It must have seemed like a dream to be trusted and respected again and to see himself moving toward destiny again in some fashion. But now this ... . Was all of that upward struggle for nothing? He had taken three steps forward, only to now take five steps back? He was now in a dungeon, lower than he had been in the beginning of this ordeal. This was a bitter blow. Could he rise from this one?

God Eclipsed the Enemy

If you understand that Satan had used Mrs. Potiphar, you will also understand that God was still in control. Mrs. Potiphar's intention was, in no way, simply to have Joseph imprisoned. No! She wanted him to die. And, more likely than not, she wanted him to die a painful death. But although God may not stop your enemies from coming against you, He will only let them go so far.

The Bible shows us that Satan seeks permission from God to *"sift [us] as wheat"* (Luke 22:31). This means Satan can only go as far as God allows him to. Think about the time you searched with frustration for your car keys, only to find them in a place you were sure you had already looked. That may have been orchestrated by God. God Himself may have blinded your eyes from seeing those keys, because of some attack Satan had planned against you on the freeway.

You should have been right in the thick of an accident, but when it took place, you were ten minutes behind schedule. Or, perhaps you had a flat tire or suffered some other catastrophe. You can know that it was not the enemy's plan just to wound you. No, he wanted you dead. He also wanted your children dead, but God put something in your spirit, and you were praying for them at the very moment the enemy attacked.

My son Corey is one of the youth ministers at our church. On his twenty-second birthday, our church youth group went on a field trip to one of the amusement parks in the area. That evening, as I was sitting in my bedroom, I went into a state of dreaming—even though I was awake. In this state, I saw my son dead. This greatly concerned me, so I began praying. I prayed the rest of the evening and fell asleep still praying.

About three o'clock in the morning my husband awakened me to say that Corey had been hurt. He was attacked by a group of men at the park. He went to the hospital emergency room, but was released later that night.

The next morning, as my husband and I informed our church family about the incident, I told them about the daydream I had experienced. I know now that God had used it to warn me so that I would pray for my son and the rest of the group.

After the verse that speaks of Satan desiring permission to sift us as wheat, Jesus goes on to tell Peter, *"But I have prayed for you"* (Luke 22:32, NKJ). This word *prayed* is a most interesting one. It's translated from the Greek word *ekleipo*, which is akin to our word *eclipse*. An eclipse happens when one celestial body stands between us and another celestial body. When Jesus spoke these words to Peter, He was saying "Peter, even though I did not stop Satan from attacking, I stood between you and him, and I took the brunt of the blow."

This is what God did for Corey, and it's exactly what He does on a daily basis for us with lost keys, flat tires, and tainted food you might eat at some restaurant. He doesn't stop the enemy's attacks, but He surely eclipses them. You may want to stop complaining and begin praising God for the awesome love and power He has shown to you:

… And having done all, to stand. Stand therefore … .

Ephesians 6:13-14

In time, Joseph came to the conclusion that God had been in all of it. After all, why hadn't he been killed? That was the punishment for a rapist, and his accusation had come directly from the wife of a high-ranking official.

But when Potiphar settled down from his initial anger over the situation, it appears that God had spoken to his heart. He may have reminded the man of what he had seen in Joseph's character throughout the years and what he had seen in his wife's. Potiphar must have somehow seen that Joseph was not capable of this crime. Why else would he have spared his life?

Poor Joseph! Even if Potiphar did believe his story, he still had to save face, so he could not release him. At least he didn't take his life. God still had purpose for Joseph. God had established his purpose in the heavenlies, and there was nothing that Potiphar, Mrs. Potiphar, or hell could do to stop Joseph.

In fact, Joseph himself was the only one who could have stopped the dream. Had he given in to Mrs. Potiphar's demands, in all likelihood he would have aborted his dream by his own hand. Because he decided to take a stand for his faith, even though he was now in prison, he was still in possession of the dream.

Don't abort your dream. We have seen many mighty man and women do this. When they confess, God still uses them, but one cannot help but think of the heights they may have attained if they had done as Paul exhorted, *"and having done all, to stand. Stand ... ."*

As we will see later Joseph, was a type of Christ. Jesus would have aborted His destiny had He sinned, and so would Joseph.

This, too, would pass. God had a plan. Joseph had paid the price of purpose. God would now use this to continue his preparation for destiny. In the meantime, prison would serve Joseph as another opportunity to sharpen the gifts he would one day need to fulfill that dream. God knew just when to intervene, and until that moment arrived, Joseph had to trust that God had his best interests at heart.

CHAPTER 12

When Facts Fight Faith

There are times in life when we face one trial after another. This can be very discouraging, especially when it appears that we have not completely come out of the last trial when the new one appears. What do you do during these times? How do you hang on during seasons when one trial after another after another presents itself?

Stripped Again!

For the second time, Joseph had now been stripped. First, his brothers had stripped him of his coat of many colors, and now he had been stripped of his hard-earned position by Mrs. Potiphar. This stripping was hard; maybe even harder than the first one. Yet, this is just a picture of what each of us goes through on our way to purpose. Life has a way of stripping us, and God allows this stripping to take place. This is because, whether we know it or not, each time we're stripped, it can actually be used for our good.

God has a desire for us to fulfill our purpose, but because our purpose is about Him and not about us, it often becomes necessary for Him to allow us to be stripped of ourselves to teach us this truth. Sometimes many layers of "us" have to be stripped away to make us usable for our purpose.

As you have journeyed through life, have you seen people who are filled with talent and ability, and yet they don't go very far? I'm talking about people of seemingly unequaled talent in their given field, who don't achieve greatness in that field, or, if they do, it is short lived. Often, this is because they perform the given action for themselves and for their glory. It is not done to help God or other people.

Such people are full of themselves. They love the fame, the praise, the recognition, and the credit. They live for their own glory. People like these are their own worst enemy. They don't need others to stop them or hinder them. They do a wonderful job of this all by themselves.

How many movies have been made about egotistical athletes, singers, entertainers, actors, and politicians? In each of these stories, the people end up falling and friendless because of their own egos. If they eventually learn that what you do in life for others is what matters most, they become better people.

Sometimes the problem of egotism is obvious. But there are times when you're around people who say all the right things at the right time, yet something about them just doesn't sit well with you. You know that something is wrong here, but you can't quite put you finger on the problem. All you know is, as the old folks used to say, "That baby don't cry right."

Usable for Purpose

Often times, in spite of a person's massive ego, he or she truly desires to be used by God. God, in love, will then allow them to go through situations and circumstances to make them usable and fulfill that desire. This often entails stripping of attitudes. These may be attitudes of pride and arrogance, not listening to others, always thinking we're right, thinking that the problem is always someone else and never us, attitudes of continually having to have things done our way and in our strength. These may be attitudes of conceit, deceit, criticism, and negativity, attitudes or beliefs passed on to us by family members and our past associations, attitudes of indifference, prejudice, apathy, dishonesty, jealousy and of half-heartedly doing things. There are a myriad of attitudes that can work against us and keep us from fulfilling God's destiny for us. And so, as stated earlier, God, in love and with purpose in view, allows these attitudes to be stripped from us, for our own good.

It is evident that Joseph needed to be stripped. Most of the time, the areas in which we need to be stripped are not so evident (to us at least). They are usually clear to our family members and associates. Even as there was a purpose each time Joseph was stripped, when you go through periods of stripping, realize God *will* use this for your good and the good of His Kingdom. Make it your goal to come through the times of stripping a better person, one who is better prepared for purpose.

That is often easier said than done. During these seasons, facts often begin to fight faith. Joseph sat in jail, once again terribly wounded. He looked around that dismal place, and he could not understand.

He thought about the dreams given all those years before. What a joyous time that had been in his life! Would he never again feel such joy? he wondered. This whole scenario needed to be sorted out. The facts were fighting with his faith.

Maybe he had gotten it all wrong. Maybe the dreams weren't from God at all. His brothers, after all, had treated him so badly. Maybe he had made the whole thing up in his mind, just to give himself some sort of peace.

No! he argued within himself. The dreams had been given by God. Dreams were God's special way of revealing Himself to His people. And his dream had been given two times, meaning that it was established. Still, he reasoned, since that time, it seemed as if all that he had experienced was heartache and delay.

Surely it was not reasonable to continue believing that God would somehow intervene for him. Things had gone from bad to worse, and no one had helped him. Up until now, people and circumstances had continually been against him. What made him think that tomorrow would be any different than today?

I'm Tired of Holding On

Many of you can identify with Joseph. There are times in life that reason, logic, and rationale cause us to want to give up. You've been holding on and hoping for such a long time, but now you're just tired. You've been praying for years for that man to change, but there's no outward evidence that it will happen. You've been hoping your finances will change, but they're worse now than when you started praying. The situation on the job has also gone from bad to worse. You don't know how you're going to make it through four more years with your child (or children).

You think to yourself, *They* can't wait until they graduate? *I* can't wait until they graduate. They're threatening *me* about leaving as soon as they graduate? Oh how I wish that graduation day were tomorrow. You smile as you picture yourself standing at the door with their suitcase, and a one-way ticket to anywhere.

There are times in life when we do all we can to alleviate certain situations, but too often, like Joseph, we find that things are beyond our control. We get to the place that we throw our hands up and don't know whether to cry or be angry. All we know is that we're T-I-R-E-D.

We're tired of holding on to some idiotic dream that things are going to get better. We realize we've been foolish for holding on as long as we have. After all, how much clearer can the situation get before we accept the fact that nothing is going to change. And when we reach this point, we give up.

Prisoners of Hope

When we decide to give up on our dreams, something happens. The day the dream was planted in our heart was a joyous day. Just like Joseph, we began hoping, looking to the day the dream would be fulfilled. That hope carried us through some disappointing times. Through it all, we held on to hope. "It will get better," we told ourselves. "The dream will come to fruition."

Even when we occasionally put the dream aside, it was never very far from the forefront of our mind, always ready and willing to remind us of its presence. But the time comes when we realize that not only has it not happened; we must finally accept the fact that it won't happen. In this way, we decide to let go of the hope that has sustained us for so long.

But, just as you give up and begin walking away from hope, a strange thing then happens. Something seizes you. You look around and realize that hope has now taken hold of you. The same hope you held on to for so many years now refuses to let go of you. You have suddenly become a prisoner of hope.

I would like to believe this is what happened to Joseph during those early days in prison. I believe that hope took hold of him and reminded him that his dream had been established in heaven. The only thing his brothers and Mrs. Potiphar had succeeded in doing was delaying the inevitable. The dreams would come to fruition. God would see to that.

> *The same hope you held on to for so many years now refuses to let go of you. You have suddenly become a prisoner of hope.*

Surviving Life

If you are a prisoner of hope, and cannot seem to let go of your dream, allow me to give you a word of encouragement on how to make it to your place of purpose sanely, without committing suicide, and without committing murder. First, you cannot wait for events to change to survive life. Your situation might not change, and you may have to deal with that fact. But, although God might not change your situation, He can change you!

Even when all of the facts war against your faith, you can still hold fast. You can be honest and tell God, *"Lord, I believe; help thou mine unbelief"* (Mark 9:24). You choose to hold on to God even if you don't see Him and believe even if the heavens are silent.

God is still on the throne. You can choose to believe that He is the God of the impossible, and that He has His own timetable. You can choose to continue to hold fast to His words of promise. You can choose to say, "He may not come when I want Him to, but He's always one time." If you choose to do this, you'll no longer allow people or circumstances to keep you from experiencing life.

Jesus said, *"I am come that they might have life, and that they might have it more abundantly"* (John 10:10). Our God does not want us simply marking time though life, as one of the living dead. He wants us to experience life, a life of prosperity, purpose, and joy.

For years, church folks of our grandparents' generation sang a song that says, "This joy that I have: the world didn't give it, and the world can't take it away." A man (or a woman) is not the source of your joy. A job is not the source of your joy. Your friends are not the source of your joy. Learn to be content in every situation—even if the world seems to be crumbling around you. God is with you, so hold on to Him and to His promises for your life. When storms are raging all around you, hold on.

Your joy and your peace are your choice. Those two things are so precious that you cannot afford to allow any person or any situation to control them. These are priceless commodities. So hold on to them at all costs. Nothing in life is worth losing your joy and peace over. Nothing!

Bloom Where You're Planted

All of the things that Joseph now faced had to be encountered, confronted, and conquered in the process of his purpose. And God was using each one of them to prepare him for that purpose.

Before he ruled Egypt, Joseph had to learn to rule himself, he had to learn to rule Potiphar's household, and now he had to learn to rule a prison. There, he would encounter others who were mistreated and unjustly accused, others who were disillusioned and disappointed with life. There he would come face to face with others who had been stripped of everything dear to them. There was a purpose for Joseph in prison.

Only God could now make the impossible happen and bring Joseph's dreams to reality, and He would do this only when Joseph was ready. This jail was just another stop on his journey to purpose. It was not the way Joseph or most anyone else would have chosen, but God knew what He was doing.

There in the prison, Joseph could have sat and sulked in his cell, and who could have blamed him? But he refused to be consumed with anger, bitterness, and resentment, and, as a result, God's presence was with him—even in that dark and evil place.

You, too, may not be happy with your current situation, especially if it's not what God has shown you. But this may be His way of getting you to your place of purpose, so don't despise it. God wanted Joseph in the palace, but he would go there by way of the slave market, the house of Potiphar and the royal prison. It wasn't the way he had chosen, but it was as good as any other way.

If you cannot be, at the moment, exactly where you want to be, then you have to learn how to prosper where you are. In prison Joseph, at last, experienced peace. Life was not passing him by. Opportunity was not being lost. He was where God wanted him, and he would prosper in those surroundings. If he could not be where he wanted to be, he would bloom where he was planted. And, when God was ready for him to be someplace else, he would get out of that prison. He was sure of it.

Joseph maintained his peace and faced each new day one at a time. If he had been like most of us, he would have developed a bad attitude somewhere along the way. But he could not afford to be angry, bitter, resentful, or vengeful at any juncture. He had a dream, and he had to get to the place of that dream. The dream was precious. If this was the price he had to pay to see it fulfilled, it was worth it.

Experiencing "Good" Pain

I was on my treadmill one day some years ago, talking to God, when tears began flowing down my face. After experiencing a few very wonderful months, I had one of life's painful experiences.

That day, as the tears flowed down my face, I realized the pain I was experiencing was a good thing for me. It would help me minister in the future. So, I made two decisions: (1) To refuse to wallow in self-pity, and (2) To learn something from my tears that could help others who were hurting.

I asked God, "Lord, let me remember this pain. The day will come that I will need to give a word of comfort to someone in despair. When that happens, I want to be able to recall these feelings." Being alone, with no one to encourage me, I then prayed and encouraged myself.

Lays Hands on Yourself

You need to make that same determination. You, too, may be alone, with no one to encourage you. If this is the case, you may need to encourage yourself.

You may not be able to get into someone's prayer line or to find someone who can help you. If you want your life to make a difference, you have to learn to get control over your own needs, so that you can concentrate on the needs of others.

I often encourage people not to wait for someone to come along, lay hands on them, and pray for them. Instead, I encourage them to learn to pray and lay hands on themselves.

In church, people often go to the altar for prayer. There, they are anointed with oil, and a minister lays his or her hands on their head or on their place of pain, and prays for them. But you might be in a situation in which you simply can't wait until Sunday to have someone pray for you. This is the reason you need to learn to pray and lay hands on yourself.

"God is no respecter of persons" (Acts 10:34). He has honored the prayers of many others, and He will honor your prayer too. Go to the kitchen and get yourself some oil. It can be olive oil or cooking oil. Pray over that oil, and then anoint yourself with it, and expect Him to heal you. The power is not in the particular oil you use. The oil just represents the Holy Spirit and His power. So try it, and you'll be blessed.

You can do this right now. I challenge you to lay hands on yourself and then encourage yourself! Pray for victory. If God did it for Joseph, He'll do it for you too, for He is still *"no respecter of persons"* today in the twenty-first century.

A Good Man Falls Seven Times, and Gets Back Up

There in that prison, days, weeks, months, and years passed. Joseph's deliverance did not come overnight. For years, he seemed to do only mundane things. During this time he continued to maintain his integrity and sharpen his gifts for what he knew was ahead. Although he had gone back to the bottom, Joseph worked hard and God honored this. He gradually worked his way up, and eventually his conscientious service came to the attention of the keeper of the prison.

The keeper of the prison liked this young man. He liked his attitude. And there was something about him that set him apart from the others. He didn't quite know what it was, but whatever it was, he decided he would keep his eye on the young man:

But the Lord was with Joseph, and shewed him mercy, and gave him favor in the sight of the keeper of the prison. And the keeper of the prison committed to Joseph's hand all the prisoners that were in the prison; and whatsoever they did there, he was the doer of it. The keeper of the prison looked not to any thing that was under his hand; because the Lord was with him, and that which he did, the Lord made it to prosper.

Genesis 39:21-23

That "something different" the keeper of the prison saw in Joseph was the favor of God. Although Joseph had lost favor with Potiphar, he had not lost favor with God. God had continued to show him favor, and the keeper saw this. That favor would now take Joseph to the place of prominence—in spite of his imprisonment.

Get Back Up Again

When my sons were young children, I purchased a clown punching bag for them. The base of this bag was filled with sand. No matter how many times they punched that clown, it would get back up. That's a great picture of Joseph. Since the age of seventeen, life had brought him much disappointment and disillusionment, but in spite of it all, each time something had knocked him down, he had gotten back up. Prison was no different. Although he was given despicable tasks, he faithfully completed each one.

If you believe that God has a great purpose for you, show Him that you can be faithful in the little things, and He will promote you. When someone knocks you down (and it will happen), be like that clown. Get back up and go on.

Don't waste your time wondering why it happened or when things will change. Just keep your eyes open and make the best of every opportunity. Try doing what Paul taught, heaping coals of fire upon the heads of those who offend you:

Therefore if thine enemy hunger, feed him; if he thirst, give him drink: for in so doing thou shalt heap coals of fire on his head. Be not overcome of evil, but overcome evil with good.

Romans 12:20-21

For those who have lost spouses, get up and go on. Start a ministry for those who have suffered the same hurts and pains, and leave your future with God. What you're going through may be the price of your purpose.

Joseph was given more and more responsibility, as the keeper of the prison grew to greatly trust and depend on him. At the same times, he began to recognize the many blessings he was receiving because of this young Hebrew. Whatever area of administration or need that was put under Joseph's supervision soon began to prosper. It was as if the young Joseph had the Midas touch.

In addition to the great job he was doing in the prison, I would imagine that Joseph personally blessed the jail keeper, or warden. Again, one of the reasons God allowed Joseph to go to Egypt in the first place was for him to bring the knowledge of God to Egypt. He had done that in Potiphar's house, and now he did the same thing in prison. More than likely Joseph often spoke of His God, calling Him the God of Abraham (his great-grandfather). The warden may have even begun to look forward to these stories.

Just being around Joseph seemed to do something positive for him. Over the years, he became quite fond of Joseph and invested him with more and more responsibility. In fact, he entrusted Joseph with such great authority that eventually the responsibility of all the prisoners was under his care. Joseph was running the prison. Then one day a new opportunity knocked at his door; an opportunity to shine. When it came, Joseph was ready.

CHAPTER 13

———⊷◦⊰———

The Eyes Are the Mirror of the Soul

Heaven has a timetable, so we would do well to learn how to tell time. Joseph was in training for purpose. This training required that he complete certain courses before he could proceed to fulfilling that purpose.

If You Want to Learn It, You Need to Live It

When God chose not to intervene on Joseph's behalf and expose Mrs. Potiphar, He had Joseph's purpose in mind. Though it may have appeared that Joseph had taken a step backward, he had actually graduated to a higher level of training. This next level of training would include several courses in the study of prison management.

My second son Christopher graduated from the University of Southern California a few years ago with a degree in International Relations. Chris is highly competitive, and when he determines that he will rule in some area, he does it—no matter how hard, and no matter what it takes. Chris is about to enter law school, and I often say that if I ever need a lawyer, he'll be my secret weapon.

155

I still remember the Christmas we got our first computer. It had some games with it, and Chris became interested in one game in particular. One day, after winning that game, his name was revealed on the screen as the champion. He loved that and continually looked for new opponents to challenge. His brothers, his friends, or anyone else who visited us became fair game for him.

Still, something bothered Chris. Each time he opened the game, more than just his name appeared. The name of the top five contender's would appear. Although he won some of the time, obviously he did not win *all* of the time, and so his was not the only name to appear on the screen. This did not sit well with him; he wanted all five spots on the list of champions. He could not countenance anyone else's name appearing as his equals on that coveted screen.

All during that Christmas season, he was on that computer from early in the morning until late at night working at that game, and six days later, he had done it. Each time the game opened, all five champions bore the name Chris Singleton.

When Chris went on to college this I-can-do-anything attitude reappeared. It utterly amazes me how young people can accomplish anything if *they* want it.

When Chris had still been in high school, it seemed to me, as his mother, that his greatest goal was to see how many classes he could skip on any given day. He would actually come up with some unique, well-thought-out excuses to accomplish this goal. Then, soon after he had graduated, it seemed that some sort of light flashed on in his head one day.

Suddenly, for no apparent reason, he cleaned his room. Then, he enrolled in community college and, much to our shock, qualified for the dean's list his first semester. He continued to earn this honor each semester, and at the end of two years, determined that he would go to the University of Southern California.

He did everything himself, and only when the acceptance process was complete and all the paperwork in place, did he inform his father and me of his intentions. After all, someone needed to pay for his classes.

Although Chris had barely survived Spanish in high school, he decided on the International Relations Program and that Spanish would be his second language. He then set out to master Spanish. After taking classes for a year, he made the decision that the best way to learn Spanish would be to live it. Thus, he took his studies to Nicaragua, and then on to Venezuela for over a year. He knew that if he really wanted to master Spanish, he needed to be in a place where that was the only language spoken, a place where he could not rely on his knowledge of English to help him communicate.

I remember, on one occasion, wanting to see how he was faring. I called the home he was staying in. The mother of the house spoke no English, and I spoke no Spanish. During the conversation, all we could both communicate to each other was *Chris* and *mama*. We were both thankful that Chris walked in while this *conversation* was in progress.

Today, we proudly listen, as Chris speaks flawless Spanish. On ministry trips, I have actually gotten him on the phone to have him communicate some thought that I was unable to communicate myself, to some Spanish-speaking person. Again, it is amazing what we can do when we want to.

Why Am I Here?

As we study this account of Joseph's prison years, we see that God ordained this time. Although Joseph's prison years were painful ones, they were also necessary years.

Let me take a moment to discuss something that seems to often go unnoticed in Joseph's story. When Joseph went to prison, the Bible says he was put in *"a place where the king's prisoners were bound"* (Genesis 39:20).

Joseph's initial time in prison was not just spent with any type of prisoner; it was spent with those who had, in some way, threatened or offended the Pharaoh. This would have included all types of prisoners practicing white-collar, as well as more threatening, crimes.

Some of these men may have inadvertently angered Pharaoh, while others may have been accused of plotting his murder or overthrow, or of having posed some other threat to his kingdom. Whatever their case, Egypt was the greatest kingdom in the then-known world, and Pharaoh was omnipotent there. No one crossed him and got away with it, and no one questioned his word once he gave it. Until further word came from the palace, these Egyptian government officials remained in prison.

Before being banished to prison, some of these officials would have been very involved in the affairs of the kingdom. These men unknowingly became Joseph's professors in his course on "governmental affairs." Under their tutelage, Joseph received much knowledge in business transactions, government dealings, and interactions, and associations and allies of the kingdom—past and present. All of the information Joseph received from these men throughout the years would one day be used to help him fulfill that which he had been sent to Egypt to do.

As we look back on Joseph's story, we now know the importance of this training from his prison professors. There is a great lesson for each of us to learn from this. When we're going through seasons of adverse circumstances, it behooves us to ask ourselves, "Why am I here? And what would God have me to learn from this situation?" We should try to resolve within ourselves the fact that this situation can be used in our future—if we are able to learn its lessons today.

During his years in prison, Joseph also learned that he was not the only one who was suffering. He encountered many other suffering individuals. They were all around him. He was not alone, and this quickly defeated the lie of Satan that no one could possibly understand what he was experiencing. It's always surprising to us to find out just how many have suffered as we have.

This is one of the reasons I love old-fashioned testimony services at church. In those moments, we get to hear from those who have suffered and overcome. We suddenly know that we're not alone, and we are encouraged. If they overcame, we can too.

The Heartache that Nobody Sees

One morning, during his normal rounds, Joseph noticed two men who were obviously in great pain. Both of them, it turned out, had been close servants of the pharaoh, one a butler and the other a baker, and both of them had been charged with wrongdoing, dismissed from their posts, and imprisoned. Their appearance was terrible to behold that morning, and Joseph asked them what was wrong. Amazingly, Joseph had now forgotten his own sufferings and was concentrating on the sufferings of others. Seeing them in such distress caused him to approach them—even though they did not verbally express their anxiety.

I guess we could say that besides being the top prison administrator, Joseph now also operated in the role of prison Chaplain. This is what Christian ministry is all about, and nothing could be more rewarding. When you give yourself to meet the needs of others, God never forgets you. Your needs will be met too.

When God brings you into contact with other people, it's often so that their needs can be met.

Many of us are so consumed by our own needs that we fail to recognize the needs of others around us. We are so focused on our own pain that we can't even think about the pain others might be suffering. If this is true, then the enemy will try to keep you in constant pain so that you can't think about anything else.

When God brings you into contact with other people, it's often so that their needs can be met. If you're unable to see or sense those needs, how can they be helped?

Earlier I told the story of my season of bitterness. During this time. I used to hope someone would look past my plastic smile and see my private pain. So many people around us experience the heartache that nobody sees that it behooves us to ask God to give us spiritual eyes, spiritual ears, and spiritual hearts, so that we can recognize the signs of suffering in others. When you greet someone and say to them, "How are you?" and they answer, "I'm fine, thank you," you need to be able to see beyond those polite surface words and to know the truth about the person's need. Is the smile on their face real or is it plastic?

We need to ask God to give us a spirit of discernment. Then, when we have seen people's true need, we can render what is needed—a hug, a word of encouragement, or whatever else seems appropriate at the time.

Sometimes we become so wrapped up in our worship services that we don't notice that someone in our midst is suffering terribly. Some are shouting exuberantly, but others are just standing there, feeling all alone and abandoned. Yet we rarely ever turn to see what's wrong with them. We just go on doing our own thing.

The medical world now offers training for doctors to become iridologists, or those who study the iris of the eye with the intent of diagnosing diseases.

With years of training, they can become experts at this. Many patients, whose conventional doctors have been unable to diagnose their particular problem, have found freedom from pain and the anxiety of not knowing their ailment by visiting these doctors who are trained to spot the not so obvious.

As for me, because of my experience in life, on Sunday mornings I now try to look into people's eyes and spot sorrow that is not obvious to everyone. I know from experience that the eyes are the mirrors of the soul. People's words may cover their true feelings, but their eyes always tell the truth.

If someone's eyes are shouting "help me," I want to hear those words in my spirit man. There are times that I'll even ask a person to take off their sunglasses as I talk to them. I tell them, "I want to see your eyes."

The $156-Million-Dollar Man

Joseph was now, in a sense, a spiritual iridologist. He had overcome his own hurt and despair to the point that he could now minister to others.

He had grown up thinking that life was all about him, and he probably had never noticed the pain his own brothers suffered. Now, when he looked at others, he was able to see the mirror of their souls and note their need.

In a sense, Joseph took a test that day, and he passed it with flying colors. This was critical to his ultimate purpose.

The men he helped that day were prisoners like him. They had no power, no prestige. There was no money, nor anything else, to be gained by helping them. Yet, Joseph chose to help them, simply because they needed help. They needed someone to talk to. They needed someone to be there for them.

When the genius inventor, million-dollar movie producer, and legendary aviator, Howard Hughes, died, he left a man named Melvin Dummar a great deal of money for giving him a ride one night through the Nevada desert. At the time, Mr. Dummar was just being a Good Samaritan, and he didn't expect any reward for his act of kindness.

The man he picked up that night claimed to be Howard Hughes, but from his disheveled appearance, unkempt hair, and scraggly beard, to Mr. Dummar, he appeared to be a pitiful bum on his last leg. He didn't believe that the man was Howard Hughes, but he gave him the ride he needed ride.

In the early hours of the morning, he eventually dropped his passenger off in Las Vegas. Years later, when Howard Hughes died and his will was read, the truth was learned. That "hobo" had indeed been Howard Hughes, and he left Melvin Dummar a reward of $156 million dollars. How was that for a ride home? Your reward for unselfish acts of kindness may not come in the form of money, but it will come.

Not surprisingly, the Howard Hughes will was contested. In the end, his fortune was divided among twenty-two relatives, and Mr. Dummar never saw a cent of the money promised to him. But heaven recorded the act, and in time it became legend through a movie, *Melvin & Howard*, which won two academy awards. Melvin Dummar not only sold his story; he also played a part in the movie.

Director Jonathan Demme (*Silence of the Lambs*) was also blessed by Dummar's kindness to Howard Hughes. *Melvin & Howard* identified Demme as a director worth watching.

There are times when people will come to you and thank you for some kind word that you spoke to them earlier in life or for some kind deed done for them. Because you did it, not expecting anything in return, when they tell you how your actions ministered to them, often you won't even remember having done it. They remembered, and it meant the world to them.

If Joseph had not learned to take time for the "prison nobodies," he would have further delayed the realization of his purpose, for one of the men he was ministering to that morning would be responsible for his eventual release and the fulfillment of his dream. We often look to people of money or power, and we don't realize that God uses the humble to achieve His purposes. It may be a homeless man on the street or a forgotten elderly person whom God uses to promote you. Yet, the "nobodies" of this world, when lifted up, can help to propel us to our place of purpose.

Despite all that he had gone through, Joseph still possessed a special gift with dreams. This gift had not diminished because of his problems. Rather, it had improved. Now he not only received dreams, but he also had the ability to interpret them. The gift now came into play.

When Joseph asked the king's butler and the king's baker what was wrong with them that morning, they told him that they had both dreamed troubling dreams and couldn't understand them. That was not a problem, he assured them. He could tell them the meaning. They proceeded to tell him the dreams, and he proceeded to tell him the interpretation of each dream.

To the butler, he said, "Three days from now you will be restored to your former trusted position," and to the baker, he said, "Three days from now you will be hanged." Three days later happened to be the pharaoh's birthday, and on that day, all that Joseph predicted came true. The baker was hanged, and the butler was restored to power.

Thinking that this might be his opportunity to be freed, Joseph asked the butler to remember him to Pharaoh, and to tell the leader of the largest world empire at the time about him, a Hebrew stolen out of his own country and forced into slavery. He was especially interested to see that the pharaoh come to know that he had been unjustly imprisoned and didn't deserve to be there. The butler said he would do just that.

In all of this, Joseph did not implicate his brothers or Potiphar's scheming wife. Most of us would have said, "My brothers did this, and my brothers did that. Potiphar's wife did this, and Potiphar's wife did that." But rather than focus on the people who had done him wrong, Joseph simply asked to be remembered. That was great wisdom. Now he awaited his answer.

God Never Forgets Us, but People Frequently Do

Since the day he had spoken those words, Joseph must have been praying especially fervent and long prayers. For the first time in years, he had a definite and specific hope within his heart that his situation would change.

One can only imagine Joseph's excitement the day the butler was released from jail. He may have wondered when he would get his audience with the Pharaoh. Joseph was sure the butler would speak to him at his first opportunity. He had helped him in his time of need. Surely he would return the good deed. He must have gone to bed full of anticipation that night.

But it was not to be. Joseph was about to learn the lesson that we all have to learn. God never forgets us, but people frequently do. Although the butler was restored, and Joseph had ministered to him and placed faith within his heart for that end, now that he was free, the man quickly forgot his promise.

There's nothing shocking about that at all. People often fail us. We pour ourselves into them, and we're there for them when they need us, but when we suddenly need *them* for something, they act as if they hardly know us. This is simply one of life's truths: people are not to be trusted; only God is.

...until God moves you, bloom right where you are.

In the days to come, every time Joseph heard the clank of the outside gate, his heart must have skipped a beat. Any day now, he expected someone to come for him.

During this time he must have asked those who knew of the comings and goings around the prison if anyone had sent a message concerning him, and when he learned that they had not, I'm sure that he was very disappointed. We get into our heads the manner in which we expect God to do things, and when He doesn't do them exactly that way, we get disappointed, discouraged, and even confused. But He is God, and He does things as it pleases Him. He does them in His own time and in His own way.

Joseph may have been expecting that the intervention of the butler would lead to him having a fair trial or at least to having his side of the issue considered. But nothing of the sort happened. He was forgotten.

As days turned into weeks, weeks into months, and months into years, it became increasingly obvious that the man he had put his hopes in had forgotten him, and that none of his expectations would come to pass. Still, Joseph had to somehow go on living, and there was no purpose in him becoming bitter. There was work to do in the prison, and he would do it. He would continue to bloom where he was planted, and when God wanted him out of that prison, He would get him out—somehow.

The Final Test of Waiting

Oh, friend, until God moves you, bloom right where you are. The soil where you're planted seems strangely unfavorable. It may be dry and lacking in nutrients. But God can supply you water and fertilizer. Just go ahead and bloom right now where you are. If it's not a good location, your blooming will seem all the more remarkable.

When the fullness of time arrives your dream will be fulfilled. Until that moment, it's just not time. Through the years, I've been very encouraged by the words of Psalm 1:

> *Blessed is the man that walketh not in the counsel of the ungodly, nor standeth in the way of sinners, nor sitteth in the seat of the scornful. But his delight is in the law of the Lord; and in his law doth he meditate day and night. And he shall be like a tree planted by the rivers of water, that bringeth forth his fruit in his season; his leaf also shall not wither; and whatsoever he doeth shall prosper.*

> Psalm 1:1-3

Your *"season"* of fruitfulness will come. God has been preparing you for it, and in time, He will honor your faithfulness.

But timing is everything. If God wants you in one particular place, He knows why, and He knows the precise moment when you're ready to move on. Let Him do His work in you. He will tell you when it's time to move on. And, at that time, He'll provide the means for you to do so.

When it's your time, nothing and nobody will be able to stop you. The enemy might succeed in delaying your dream, but only if you cooperate with him. Without your help, he's powerless.

God is even now robing you in royal garments to prepare you for your day. Choose to cooperate with Him, and that day will be hastened.

Friend, what grade are you getting in the course of life? What's your score on the test of pain? And how are you doing in the great test of waiting? It seems that a lack of patience is what afflicts most Christians these days, and they're overcome by the waiting test. Most of us prefer being in the middle of some storm to just waiting. We hate waiting—anywhere and for anybody. Now, Joseph just had to wait.

God doesn't do things on our timetable. We don't know when we're ready for purpose. Only He knows, so only He can set the proper time.

"When, Lord?" we ask so often. But no answer comes. Instead, God simply urges us to trust Him. He knows when the time is right.

CHAPTER 14

Hidden Until the Time of Purpose

When Joseph's hopes were dashed, he could have become angry and bitter over this failure on the part of a man he had helped. After all, Joseph had been there at the butler's time of need. Now, the butler was ungrateful and had forgotten him. But noticing the pain of someone else and ministering to their need proved, in time, to be his ticket to freedom. It hastened the arrival of his day of destiny. Had he not done it, he would no doubt have stayed in that prison much longer.

As it was in Joseph's case, we, too, cannot afford to become resentful when people fail to take the time to thank us properly, or when they simply forget us. People are not always appreciative, but we're called to help them anyway. They don't always respond positively, but we're expected to assist them nevertheless. Even if we receive no recognition, no thanks, and no reward, we're still called to help other people, and God requires that we do it. Still, you never know how a kindness you do today might bring you reward in the future.

Givers and Takers

It was only at the end of two full years, years that must have seemed like the longest Joseph could ever remember having endured, that his elevation came. It finally happened, and it happened in this way.

Pharaoh had a dream, a dream that was so real that he could find no peace and no rest until he understood it. He sought help on every hand, but no one seemed capable of interpreting the dream.

This was not unusual. People often look for help in all the wrong places, when the help they need just may come from somewhere else entirely.

It was only after Pharaoh had exhausted all other avenues of possible help that the butler remembered Joseph. If anyone could interpret the Pharaoh's dream, he could. He was sure of it, and he recommended him to Pharaoh.

The butler now must have felt very ashamed that Joseph had helped him, and yet he had forgotten to help Joseph in return. Each of us needs to become more thankful in life—both to God and to the people He uses to help us along life's way. Ungrateful people don't get very far in life.

A thank-you may be all that you can offer, but, if so, that's often enough. Don't ever minimize the power of gratitude, and don't fail to render it where it's due.

Many people become discouraged because no one seems to appreciate the help they're offering. We should never be guilty of contributing to the burnout sometimes experienced because of this phenomenon. Thank those to whom thanks are due.

Whatever you do, don't fail to thank God. And how can you do that? It's simple: "Thank You, Lord." Say it often, and say it from the heart. Say it in as many different ways as you can. Thank Him for anything and everything you can think of that He has done for you, and He will do more. He loves a spirit of thanksgiving in His people.

Most mornings of my life I walk through my house and tell God, "Thank You." I then thank Him for my children, and I thank Him for my husband.

When I lie down in my bed at night, I thank God that I have a bed. I'm not sure how many modern Christians do that. Yet, there are many homeless people here in America, and even more in third-world countries. I thank God for my pillow and for my blanket. Some people don't have one.

Every time I open my refrigerator to get something to eat, I thank God for a refrigerator. Many people in the poorer parts of the world don't have one.

And some have refrigerators, but they're empty. We have so much to be thankful for.

You don't always have to thank God for *doing* something. Thank Him for *being* such an awesome God, for being so loving, so merciful, and so kind. Thank Jesus for dying on the cross for you.

We are to give thanks in all things:

In every thing give thanks: for this is the will of God in Christ Jesus concerning you.

1 Thessalonians 5:18

I love songs that say thank You. Such songs of thanksgiving should be found in the heart of each of God's people. All we are and all we ever hope to be is due to His love for us. Therefore, praise should be our *"reasonable service"* (Romans 12:1). It can be given at any time of the day or night, no matter what our surroundings happen to be.

Praise, or thanksgiving, comes in many forms. One of them is giving. I'm often puzzled and perplexed by people who don't want to give to ministries that are carrying on God's work. The people in question have reaped the benefits of God's blessings, and yet they don't want to give Him anything in return. They make the mistake of thinking that they're giving to a particular organization or church, not realizing that who it goes to is just an added bonus of giving. The first and best blessing of giving is that of saying thank-you to God through our gifts.

The reason some people never reap a great harvest is that they refuse to plant seeds in God's Kingdom. We can't pray and ask God to water their seed, because they haven't planted any.

In life, there are givers (those who give and give and then give some more), and then there are the takers (those who never offer anybody anything). These are the people who think that life owes them something. They're coworkers who never offer to pay for lunch, and they're family members who can't give God two hours a week for a worship service in church. Still, when hard times come, they seem to have no problem coming to those of us who have been faithful to God ask for some of the finances He has blessed us with.

Takers are like the relatives who needed a place to stay for the weekend, and then left six months later. You fed them without getting a dime in return, and they didn't even offer to wash dishes in return. Now that they're on their feet, they don't remember your help. If they do remember, they think that you should have given your "cous" or your "bro" this help. And, God forbid that you should ever need them for anything. If you do, you'll be in trouble.

You need to ask yourself, "Am I a giver or a taker?" If you've been a taker during your lifetime, there's no time like the present to turn that around.

Thank God for your health. Thank Him that you have strength to raise your hands in praise to Him and to glorify His name. Thank Him for a sound mind and a voice to speak.

Learn to use the wonderful praise word *hallelujah*! If you speak more than one language, praise God in a second language.

Thank You For Waking Me Up Clothed in My Right Mind

Teenagers especially need to learn this lesson of simple gratitude to God. I remember, as a teenager, laughing at the older folks in the church for praying about what seemed to us foolish things. One of the elderly deacons would always say, "Thank You, Lord, that I woke up this morning clothed in my right mind." As I grew older, I realized how important such a prayer was. Life throws a lot of surprises our way, and if we didn't have the Lord to help us face them, we would be in serious trouble.

You may know exactly what I mean by that. After all you've gone through, you know you shouldn't really be in your right mind. And yet you are.

If not insane, you should have, at the very least, been in prison. Somebody should have been hurt. But God held your hand, and you didn't commit murder, suicide, or any such evil. You need to thank God.

In a difficult moment of my life, my spiritual mother, Marie Brewington, challenged me, "Every night before you go to bed, take some anointing oil and anoint your temples with it, and pray, 'God, keep the rims of my mind this night.'" She understood that I was going through a hard time in my life, and I needed the Lord to protect my mind.

This is an area where we all need the Lord's intervention. If you're going through a hard season, I encourage you to pray the same prayer each night until the situation is alleviated. As long as you have your right mind, thank God for it.

Thanks comes in many forms. There is a ministry in the hug, and we need more of those these days. You should be grateful to those who have loved you enough to be willing to lift you up in any way.

You should be grateful to those who have loved you enough to be willing to lift you up in any way.

Make a phone call, pay someone a visit. Be thankful, and show your gratitude. It might be to your parents. Tell them, "Thank you for putting up with me while I was so ungrateful and immature." Thank the person who helped you get a job. Thank the person who put ten dollars in your hand when you were broke. Thank the person who gave you a hug the day you were feeling totally discouraged. God blesses the thankful heart.

Now, at last, the butler was thankful, and he remembered Joseph.

Unexpected Blessings

Many times in life, when we finally let go of our desires, they unexpectedly take place. This is, more than likely, where Joseph was at this point in his life. When Pharaoh heard about Joseph, he was excited and immediately sent for him. Joseph had to quickly bathe, shave, and change his garments, and just that quickly he was ready and set off with his escort to the palace.

What must he have been thinking about on his way there? Perhaps he concluded that the butler had finally spoken to Pharaoh, and he was about to get his long awaited audience for being wrongfully imprisoned. Was God still with him? Would he vindicate him and reveal his innocence to Pharaoh? He would soon know, for his hour had come.

The Dream and Its Interpretation

What do you do when you meet a pharaoh? What is the proper protocol? Joseph had no way of knowing for sure, although he had some knowledge from what he had learned from the king's prisoners. I'm sure he was nervous, apprehensive, and excited—all at the same time.

Was he dressed properly? Would he look out of place? Had he cut himself while shaving so quickly? There are many things that play with our minds. Joseph had to push them all aside now, and concentrate on what God would show him. His hour had come.

Formalities aside, Pharaoh told Joseph the dream, and Joseph very quickly gave him the interpretation. Nothing had hindered him through the years. His gifts were not diminished.

The interpretation of the dream was very detailed and very strange. There would be seven years of exceptionally good harvests in Egypt and the surrounding areas, but these would be followed by seven years of exceptionally poor harvests. The suffering in the poor years would be so terrible that the good years would quickly be forgotten.

Most of us have experienced something similar. We, too, have good years and bad years. Often, the bad years seem endless—almost interminable, and during this time we, too, sometimes forget the good years we previously experienced. But nothing is forever. During times of trial, we must adopt the attitude, "This, too, will pass." The trials God sends our way are just for a certain season, and then they're gone and can be forgotten. They may seem like they will go on forever, but they won't.

Just as with everything else, there's a time to go into a trial, and there's a time to come out. There's a time for preparation, and there's a time for ruling. It was clearly Joseph's time.

Joseph not only interpreted Pharaoh's dream; he also offered a formula for prosperity during the coming famine. During the good years, every Egyptian was to bring one fifth of his harvest into Pharaoh's storehouse.

As believers, we need to be storing up the treasures of the Word of God in our hearts, so that in times of spiritual drought we can stay alive, and also so that others who are experiencing famine can come to us for help. I am strong in the Word of God today because, during my own times of suffering, I drew closer to Him.

During some periods, I felt that there was no earthly person upon whom I could call for help. I was forced to turn to the Lord. In my desperation, I devoured

His Word, reading it morning, noon, and night, and allowing it to speak to me and calm my wounded spirit. As a result, now, when someone else is in famine and they come to me for help, I always have a spiritual feast for them.

In this same way, other people should be able to come to you, no matter what situation they find themselves in, and know that you will have an answer for them. This is especially important for those who are in youth ministry today. Young people have many questions. They have hurts that need to be nursed, and they have empty places that need to be filled. If God gives you the opportunity to minister to young people, be sure that you're filled and ready to pour into their lives. Always have a fresh word to sow into them. Store up in good times for these times of need.

Elevated to the Place of Purpose

As Joseph stood before Pharaoh, he further recommended that Pharaoh place someone responsible, an administrator, over this whole operation to make sure the collection effort went smoothly.

Pharaoh was enormously relieved. Although the interpretation had not brought with it the best news, God gave him peace in his heart. He was so moved by Joseph's wisdom that he now honored him. The fact that he was a slave, an ex-prisoner, and a man hated and rejected by his own family had not stopped God from blessing him in the past, and now He was doing it again.

Joseph's words found favor with Pharaoh. As he listened and watched this young Hebrew confidently map out a plan to keep his kingdom prospering, Pharaoh pondered within himself who could take on such a massive endeavor.

Evidently the royal advisors had fallen out of favor, perhaps because they could not interpret the Pharaoh's dream. Whatever the case, God used the situation to elevate Joseph.

Pharaoh thought that Joseph would be perfect for the position:

And Pharaoh said unto his servants, Can we find such a one as this is, a man in whom the spirit of God is? And Pharaoh said unto Joseph, Forasmuch as God hath showed thee all this, there is none so discreet and wise as thou art: Thou shalt be over my house, and according unto thy word shall all my people be ruled: only in the throne will I be greater than thou. And Pharaoh said unto Joseph, See, I have set thee over all the land of Egypt.

Genesis 41:38-41

How phenomenal that a Hebrew slave who had been doing time in prison was placed in such a position of responsibility—and without any lengthy period of consideration! Pharaoh did not first consult with his advisors and glean their collective wisdom on the subject. He just told them what he intended to do, and then he did it.

I am positive that if Pharaoh had given his officials the opportunity, they would have blocked Joseph's promotion. He may have actually been simply told thank-you and returned to his prison cell.

There are many times in which a person in leadership must take a stand and do what *"thus saith the Lord"* in spite of others that may be under them. If Joshua had taken a vote, the children of Israel would have stayed on the wrong side of the Jordan River until the waters subsided. Then, they would have missed out on a great miracle.

The same holds true for Jericho. This is probably one reason God commanded the people not to say a word as they "foolishly" marched around the walls of that city. There was no complaining, no second guessing the leader, and no comments, for instance, that Moses had never done it this way. And because Joshua took a stand without taking a vote, seven days later, the walls of the strongest fortress in Canaan fell through the use of the weapon of the shout.

That same day that Joseph met the Pharaoh he became Prime Minister of Egypt, second only to Pharaoh in command and in respect. He would ride in the second chariot, and all men would bow the knee to him. In recognition of this, Pharaoh placed a golden necklace around Joseph's neck and a special ring on his finger, and he had him dressed in royal garments.

Pharaoh also gave Joseph a new name, Zaphnath-paaneah, and a suitable wife, Asenath the daughter of Potipherah, priest of On. Together, Joseph and Asenath would have two wonderful sons. What more could a man ask for?

When God initially gave Joseph his dreams, he was seventeen years old. Since that time, he had lived a life of suffering. He had suffered the painful separation from his father, the painful rejection of brothers, the fear of the pit, the pain of being sold into slavery, as well as the rigors of slavery. He had suffered the humiliation of being labeled a rapist, years in prison, and the suffering time and delays in general bring. Joseph was now thirty. It had taken thirteen years for the dreams to come to fruition. But they did come to fruition. All of Egypt now bowed down to him.

Hidden Until the Time of Purpose

We would be wrong to suppose that there was no one in the kingdom who opposed Joseph's promotion or gave him a hard time. That often happens when someone seems to come out of nowhere and is suddenly elevated. But God had kept Joseph hidden until the time of his purpose.

Joseph was elevated in a single day, but in spite of the fact that he had seemingly come out of nowhere, he was well qualified for the position. All of the blessings Pharaoh gave him that day had come only after a very long and arduous period of preparation, but now the period of preparation was over, and Joseph was ready to rule.

The pit and the dungeon could be forgotten, but never the lessons Joseph learned there. Everything he had passed through along the way had been for the purpose of his preparation and had served him well. But now he was ready.

Most of us have seen God do this over and over again in His Kingdom. Often He keeps His delegates hidden and out of controversy from the public's view while He prepares them for great purposes. When the time comes, they, too, appear out of nowhere to places of honor. Often, as was the case of Joseph, people who see this become jealous and unsupportive. How sad! God has purpose for us all. Some elevation to purpose takes place in view of the public, and some takes place in obscurity. Still, if we're walking in our God-ordained purpose, He will be glorified. Because of this, we need to avoid falling into Satan's trap of jealousy and do all that we can to support each other.

It was now Joseph's time, and the horrors of the past could now be forgotten. It was time for elevation.

When the people heard about this Joseph, Prime Minister of Egypt, they must have asked, "Who's Zaphnath-paaneah? I've never heard of him before." Suddenly and unexpectedly, a stranger had come on the scene.

Joseph's Sons and Their Significant Names

In one day, everything had changed. Joseph had received a position of prominence, great authority, and the respect that went with it, and Pharaoh had thrown in a wife, one of the daughters of a local priest. With her, Joseph would have two sons:

The next seven years were good ones for Joseph. His marriage to Asenath seems to have brought him joy, and his new job seems to have done the same. Now, God blessed Joseph with sons, two of them; Manasseh and Ephraim. With prison behind him and the palace in front of him, Joseph was now able to settle some issues in his heart. The names he gave to his two sons reveal to us that this took place.

Joseph named his firstborn son Manasseh meaning "forgetting" or "forgetfulness." He said:

For God...hath made me forget all my toil, and all my father's house.

Genesis 41:51

Joseph named his second son, Ephraim, meaning "two-fold increase" or "very fruitful." He said:

For God hath caused me to be fruitful in the land of my affliction.

Genesis 41:52

During those seven years, Joseph had begun to heal on the inside. He was now able to put all of the pain, misery, and sorrow of the past in the past. It was now all behind him. Because of this, he was able to prosper in a foreign land, Egypt.

For you today, know this: You may never leave Egypt, but if you look to God, you can prosper there. Before you can do this, however, you have to have a Manasseh determination. There comes a time when you must put the past in the past. If you pray to God, He can help you get to the place where you can say, "God has made me to forget." Stop complaining, and start pressing forward.

Remember, God is able to make us fruitful, but it's up to us to forget what people have done to us in the past and to recognize that just as they meant it for evil, God meant it for good.

You surely cannot afford to live your life consumed with anger.

Vengeance is Mine

It's always easier to forgive people when they recognize their error and repent of it. It's infuriating when they want to act like nothing has ever happened, or they try to make it seem like what happened was actually your fault, not theirs. But even that doesn't justify a failure to forgive. Forgive them, not so much for their sake, but for your own.

You surely cannot afford to live your life consumed with anger. It will not be easy for you to remain silent, as everyone around you thinks that this person is wonderful, when you know in your heart what they're really like. But just leave it with God and move on. He said:

To me belongeth vengeance, and recompense; their foot shall slide in due time: for the day of their calamity is at hand, and the things that shall come upon them make haste.

Deuteronomy 32:35

Dearly beloved, avenge not yourselves, but rather give place unto wrath: for it is written, Vengeance is mine; I will repay, saith the Lord. Therefore if thine enemy hunger, feed him; if he thirst, give him drink: for in so doing thou shalt heap coals of fire on his head. Be not overcome of evil, but overcome evil with good.

Romans 12:19-21

For we know him that hath said, Vengeance belongeth unto me, I will recompense, saith the Lord. And again, The Lord shall judge his people. It is a fearful thing to fall into the hands of the living God.

Hebrews 10:30-31

Choosing to Remain Where God Has Placed You

Joseph was now an honored and respected official, and, as such, he didn't have to remain in Egypt. Pharaoh would have allowed him to go back home to see his father and his brothers. But Joseph now chose to stay in Egypt because his purpose was in Egypt. At the beginning, he had surely hated Egypt and would have done anything at all to escape it. Now, God had given Egypt a special place in his heart, and he refused to leave it for any reason.

Stay where your purpose is. Stop trying to get out of that job, and stop trying to get out of that city. There is an Egypt in which God can cause you to grow and mature to the place of prosperity. Don't jump ship before your time comes.

CHAPTER 15

Everyone Gets Their Turn at Bat

A s a child, I often played baseball with friends. I was not the best at this game, but one thing did encourage me. No matter how poorly my performance was, even if I struck out, I knew I would get another turn at bat. Even if the other team was ahead, until that game ended, I knew that my team would eventually come off of the field, and everyone would get there turn at bat. It was now Joseph's turn.

During the nine ensuing years, Joseph went about his daily routine, meeting the needs of the people who came to him for help. Two years into the famine, people from all the surrounding areas began coming to Egypt to buy grain—just as Joseph had foreseen. When he had first stood before Pharaoh years before, he had advised him to save a fifth of all of Egypt's harvests during the years of plenty. This would allow them to have grain available throughout the lean years. And this had been done. The amount of grain that had been stored was so vast that it could no longer be calculated. But as the years of famine would prove, it would all be needed.

This is wise counsel for any person in any period of time. As Christians, we can learn a great lesson from this. We may tithe to God, but He views this as an act of obedience. He has told us in His Word to bring our tithes into the storehouse. This, then, is our minimum requirement. When we're faithful to do this, God, in turn, is faithful to bless us for our obedience.

But as we grow closer to God and our love for Him grows, we often find that giving a tithe is not enough to express that love. We find that it's not enough to simply give God gifts of obedience, gifts that He tells us simply prove that we're not thieves. One of the characteristics of love is that it always wants to give. A heart that is grateful to God will constrain us to go far beyond the tithe of obedience and give gifts of love.

With a gloomy outlook for our American social security system, we should begin looking to God for what our government will not be able to do for us within a few short years—give us financial security. You may be contributing to social security (as you rightfully should), but you also need to make a further investment, to store up for hard times. Try giving a fifth of your income into the King's storehouse, and then the King will provide for you in your time of famine.

"My Turn"

The ravages of the famine eventually reached Canaan. Upon hearing that there was grain in Egypt, Jacob sent his ten sons there to buy grain. One day, as the many foreigners poured into Egypt and Joseph and his staff attended to their needs, a group of ten men bowed before him. Something about them caught Joseph's attention. When they stood to their feet, he looked into their faces and realized that they were none other than his ten brothers—the same brothers who had sold him into slavery. They had changed a little, of course, but he easily recognized them.

His brothers, however, did not recognize him. After all, Joseph now looked like an Egyptian and sounded like an Egyptian. Also, as far as the brothers were concerned, Joseph was dead. As we know, he probably should have been dead. Only God's purpose upon his life and his faith in God had kept him alive.

The brothers approached him and bowed, and when they did, *"Joseph remembered the dreams"* (Genesis 42:9).

When Wounds Are Reopened

As we have seen, after Joseph became Prime Minister, he forgot his father's house and never sought permission to go back there. With the birth of Manasseh, Joseph forgot the past. That part of his life was behind him. But, in addition, it appears that during those years, Joseph had also forgotten his dreams, for you cannot *"remember"* unless you have first forgotten.

Forgetting the wrongs of the past, of course, is easier said than done. Sometimes we think that we have put a thing behind us, but in reality it has just gone into hibernation until something awakens it. Then, suddenly, something happens to cause it to rise up again and dominate our thinking. This can happen in most unusual ways.

You may be watching television, and one of the names on the list of credits sparks a memory in you. You may be driving, and the name on a street sign sparks something in you. Or maybe you hear some song from the past, and with it, comes many memories. There are many things that cause us to remember events. Sometimes these events bring a smile to our faces, and then there are those that bring pain to our hearts.

As Joseph sat and listened to his brothers' request for food, his mind wandered. He saw their lips moving, yet he did not hear their words. Instead, the dreams of the past began to flood his mind, and with them, years of forgotten pain.

Sometimes wounds only appear to be healed. When the injury first occurred, a scab formed. Eventually, the scab fell off, and a layer of new skin appeared in its place. Yet, no matter how healed some wounds may appear, underneath they can remain uncured. If something disturbs this wound, the pain felt signifies that the wound has not experienced complete healing.

I still remember the time when the mother of one of my dear friends began experiencing terrible pains in her abdomen. Reviewing her x-rays, doctors found that, unbeknownst to her, many years earlier, during surgery, a surgical instrument had been left inside of her. She had been sewed up and sent home, and her healing seemed to proceed normally.

Now, years later, after she and her family had moved to another state, she was told that the implement left in her years earlier had caused a serious infection; that infection had spread throughout her body, and, sadly, there was nothing the doctors could do. She should prepare her family for her imminent death.

Because wounds are not limited to the physical realm, we can see that this same scenario takes place with emotional, psychological, and mental wounds. We think we're past the pain, or over the person or situation—until something happens that shakes us up.

There are also times when wounds need to be reopened and cleansed, so that they can heal properly. For this woman, it was too late for that, but God was about to take Joseph through such a time.

Now, as he watched his brothers and conversed with them about the needed grain, his thoughts seemed out of control. He now remembered so vividly the day they had sold him. He had screamed, and pleaded with them in desperation. "Please don't do this, but they wouldn't listen. He had begged them, but they had just looked away. It was all coming back to him again.

Remembering the Dream

At the same time that offenses are hard to forget, it seems somehow easy to forget our dreams. This seems to have happened with Joseph. With the passage of that much time and the huge changes time had now brought to him, Joseph had let his dreams slip away.

Now, when he saw his brothers, it must have sparked in him a mixture of emotions. It would have been normal if he had immediately lashed out at them and said, "Oh, so you thought I was dead, did you? Well, look at you; you're bowing to me, just as I said you would!"

His mind must have been racing in search of some means of avenging himself against his brothers. When they had taken hold of him, stripped him, placed him in the pit, and later sold him, he had felt so powerless. They were so much bigger and stronger than he, and they outnumbered him. Now the roles were reversed. He had them right where he wanted them. He could do absolutely anything at all he wanted to with them, and no one would complain about it. In Egypt, his word was law.

If he chose to, he could torture them. He could have them killed in any number of innovative ways. He could do anything he chose to do to them, and it appears that he at least contemplated just that. But a quick death would be too kind. No, his brothers needed to suffer as he had. A plan began to form in Joseph's mind.

In the course of conversation, he learned his father Jacob was still alive, and his brothers now thought he was dead. But Joseph was far from dead, and the feelings he was experiencing certainly were not dead. He accused his brothers of being spies and said that they would be imprisoned, and then he watched them squirm. They needed to know what it was like to be falsely accused. They needed to know what it felt like to be helpless and alone. When they offered a lengthy explanation of whom they were and why they had come to Egypt, he rejected it outright and again accused them of being spies.

Next, Joseph put all of his brothers in jail and left them there for three days. Of course, they had no way of knowing how long they would be there or if they would ever be freed. They needed to know how that felt.

I Fear God

Joseph's brothers were now in jail, and were it not for his relationship with God, they could have died there. But three days later, they were suddenly released. Joseph pronounced, *"This do, and live; for I fear God"* (Genesis 42:18).

During the three days his brothers were in jail, God continued to work in Joseph's heart. Although they probably deserved to sit in jail and rot, that was not Joseph's choice to make. His brothers belonged to God and, because of that, any punishment they received would need to come from Him. Joseph quickly realized they, too, had suffered through the years.

Joseph did release his brothers, but during the past three days, as he had let go of his own plans for revenge, he had remembered his little brother Benjamin. He began to wonder if his brothers had treated young Benjamin in the same harsh manner they had treated him. With that thought in mind, he made some difficult demands on them and watched their discomfort.

First, he insisted that their missing brother Benjamin be brought as proof that they were not lying to him. With this command, the brothers became quite agitated and nervously began to converse among themselves. This was happening because of what they had done to their little brother all those years ago. They reminded each other of Joseph's anguish of soul when he begged them not to sell him.

You don't break God's laws; they break you.

Reuben chastised the others for being hard headed and reminded them that this was their fault for not listening to him concerning Joseph. He must have said, "Didn't I tell you not to sin against the boy? But you wouldn't listen! Now we must give an accounting for his blood."

They knew that Jacob would never let Benjamin out of his sight. He had lost Joseph, his beloved Rachel had died giving birth to Benjamin, and Benjamin was all that he had left to cling to.

This was a new revelation to Joseph. He never knew that Reuben had tried to come to his defense that dreadful day. As Joseph listened to them speaking in his native tongue, he also saw that his brothers had suffered years of guilt for what they had done to him. Tears welled up inside of him, and he left their presence to find a private place to weep. The wound had been reopened, so that God could now cleanse it.

Joseph would experience three times of cleansing during this spiritual surgery. The last would free him once and for all.

You Don't Break God's Laws; They Break You

You don't break God's laws; they break you. When God forbids some act, He knows that it is for our good. So, when people choose to engage in evil, they must pay the consequences—one way or another. Often, when we come against some man or woman, the actions seem justified. But if a person has some semblance of conscience, these deeds will come back to haunt them.

Conscience is a wonderful thing. It often stays our hand, and even when it doesn't, it often metes out the deserved punishment, until we make the necessary peace with God.

The Testimony of Your Conscience

Joseph figured he needed some assurance that the brothers would return, so he insisted on keeping one of them as a guarantee. He also demanded that they bring back Benjamin with them on the return trip.

Many who have studied this passage have wondered why Joseph demanded that Simeon stay behind in jail while he allowed the others to return home. It is very interesting. I personally believe that this was because of Joseph's new-found revelation from Reuben's words. Reuben was the eldest, and it had been his responsibility to look after his brothers … all of them. Even though Reuben had not used his authority and stopped his brothers from harming Joseph, Joseph now found that he had at least tried.

Simeon, the second-born son, was the oldest of the brothers who had terrorized him. With Reuben's revelation came some gratitude from Joseph, so He took Simeon from them and bound him before their eyes.

Reuben's acts teach us all that leaders need to lead. If you have authority in some area, you need to practice that authority—even if that costs you.

When I was fourteen, two friends and I were walking home one day, when we meet up with a "dorky" young girl. My two friends started harassing her and pushing her around. This was not right, and my upbringing would not allow me to participate in it. But my conscience also spoke to me that not participating was not enough; I needed to intervene on behalf of this stranger. I took the lead and began insisting that the others leave the girl alone. And I kept insisting until they did.

Although my friends did eventually listen to me and stop harassing the girl in question, they then turned their wrath on me and made fun of me for being a goody-two-shoes. But I didn't care. I knew that I had done what was right, and if this was the consequence, so be it.

During the course of them belittling me, they said these words, "If there's anything good about a person, Charlyn will see it." Although this was voiced as a slap, the remark blessed me, and, to this day, I still remember those words with pride.

The Plan to Rescue Benjamin

At the same time, Joseph did something very unusual that reveals to us the struggle that he was experiencing in his soul. One part of him wanted revenge, but another part of him wanted to demonstrate the love he still felt for his brothers.

Rather than sending them away empty-handed, he sold his brothers the provisions they sought. He then had one of his aides return the money they had paid, placing this money into the sack of each one, so that they would find it later. On their way home, one of the brothers opened his sack to get some feed for his donkey. When he discovered what had been done, they were all terrified as to what this could mean.

Upon returning to Canaan, the brothers recounted the story to Jacob with great trepidation. They had assessed the situation correctly. Jacob was furious when he learned that his sons had confided in this stranger all the details of their family, especially the fact that they had a baby brother. They tried to explain that they had been frightened by the rough treatment afforded to them by the man, whom they called *"the lord of the land"* (Genesis 42:30).

His sons informed him that this Prime Minister was next in rank to Pharaoh himself and that he insisted that they bring Benjamin to Egypt to prove to him that they were not spies. "If we don't do that, he won't release Simeon."

But Jacob would not hear of it. He had suffered enough already. Joseph was lost, and now Simeon was lost. He would not release Benjamin to them. Losing Joseph had caused Jacob far too much grief, and he could not bear the thought of losing Benjamin too. Reuben even offered to put his two sons up as a guarantee that Benjamin would be returned. He said to his father:

Slay my two sons, if I bring him not to thee.

Genesis 42:37

Even with that, Jacob refused. Simeon would just have to sit there in jail. That was the end of it. The case was closed.

As the brothers unpacked their bags, each, in turn, found his money, and they told their father about it. Now they were all frightened. What could this mean? It didn't seem to make sense.

The Cleansing Power of Tears

Tears are God's gift to man, for they provide a cleansing for the soul. In most societies, men are denied the privilege of experiencing this cleansing, but women the world over know that there's nothing quite like a good cry. Women know that after times of great tears usually comes a deep sleep, and when you awaken, it seems as if everything is better. Joseph was about to experience a second round of cleansing.

Forgotten Memories

Joseph's life changed dramatically with the arrival of his brothers, and during the months he waited for them to return with Benjamin, he began to desire to be found once again in the presence of family. God had blessed him in Egypt, he was treated kindly there (like royalty really), and even Pharaoh had grown to love him like a son, but something was missing.

Here in Egypt, his wife and children were his only family, and until now, that had been enough. But with his brothers return, the desire for family had been reawakened within him. He may not have been quite ready for fellowship with all family members, especially his older brothers, who had done him so much harm. But he now ached to see his father and, especially, for his little brother Benjamin.

Joseph's plan may have initially been filled with payback, and then with the desire to just see his brother Benjamin, but over the months, the plan evolved. Now Joseph wanted more. He wanted Benjamin to *stay* in Egypt with him.

Now, as he awaited the brothers' return, he began to look back at the events of the past twenty-two years. He now vividly remembered the dreams of his brothers and father bowing to him. In spite of his brothers evil plans to stop this, the dreams had now come to pass.

As Joseph allowed his mind to be filled with thoughts from his past, his wife Asenath must have noticed that he now spent hours walking alone on the veranda. He always seemed to be a thousand miles away. She noticed, too, that his face would often cloud over with sorrow. Sometimes she would hear him mumble some angry word. Yet, when she looked, he was alone. For whom were those words meant?

As many of us know, going back to deal with the past often brings much pain. We can choose to stay and deal with this painful past (which, though disturbing, is usually best), or we can push the past back into the past and go on. It's our choice. As for Joseph, the thoughts of the past so filled his mind that he had no choice but to at least try to settle these issues of the past in his heart.

Little Brother!

In time, the famine forced Jacob to relent and allow Benjamin to accompany the other brothers to Egypt. He warned them that if anything happened to the boy, he would hold them all personally responsible. He told them to take some special gifts for the master of Egypt, *"the best fruits," "a little balm, and a little honey, spices, and myrrh, nuts, and almonds"* (Genesis 43:11). They were also to take double money and the money that had been returned to them in their sacks, just in case it had somehow been an oversight.

When the brothers eventually arrived at Joseph's house this time, they went through a long retelling of events to his steward, in hopes of clearing their names. The steward told them not to worry and soon brought Simeon to join them. He gave them all water to wash with, and he took their pack animals and had them fed.

When Joseph arrived, he asked the men about their aging father. Then he turned his attention to Benjamin. "So this is your younger brother," he said, eyeing the lad up and down. He tried to control himself, but he clearly wasn't prepared for this moment. Just the sight of Benjamin deeply affected him. He had not seen his beloved little brother in twenty-two years. Now, he desperately wanted to grab and hug him and not let him go.

In that moment, Joseph could no longer contain himself. He abruptly rushed out of the room and barely made it to his private chambers where he began to weep. His emotions were getting the best of him, but now that he had seen Benjamin, he was more determined than ever before to see if his brothers had been traumatizing the lad as they had done him. Just that thought was enough to bring his emotions under control again. He washed his face and returned to order the banquet to begin.

Joseph could not sit beside his brothers because the Egyptians considered it an abomination to sit beside a Hebrew. But because he, too, was a Hebrew, he sat apart from his Egyptians servants.

As the banquet proceeded, Joseph sat and closely observed his brothers. They were amazed when they realized that they were seated in the order of their birth. What a coincidence!

Joseph's servants proceeded to serve the meal. When they had all been served, Benjamin's portion was larger than the others. In fact, it was five times as large. The others didn't seem to notice this, or if they did, it didn't seem to bother them. They ate and drank and were merry. This was not at all what Joseph had expected. Benjamin was the son of Jacob's beloved Rachel, even as he himself was, and yet his brothers did not appear to have the same hatred toward Benjamin as they had previously shown toward him because of it.

Early the next morning, the brothers were led to their animals that were already saddled and loaded with as much as they could carry and were allowed to begin their journey homeward. But Joseph had not finished with his plan. He was still convinced that Benjamin would be better off living with him in Egypt.

He had devised a scheme to accuse the brothers of theft and would complicate it by implicating Benjamin. He again had the money they paid for the grain returned to their sacks, but this time he also had his own personal chalice, a pure silver cup, planted in the mouth of Benjamin's sack. Then, when it seemed that time enough had elapsed for the men to have reached the outskirts of the city, he sent his trusted servant to overtake the group, accuse them of theft, and search their sacks.

The brothers were horrified. How could the lord think that they would do such a thing? They had appreciated his kindness in preparing them a feast, giving them and their animals accommodation for the night, selling them grain, and releasing Simeon to go home with them. They would never respond is such an ungrateful manner. After all, had they not brought back the money that had been found in their sacks the last time? Would they now steal from the master's house?

"If anything is found in one of our sacks," they boasted unwisely, "let the one whose sack contains it die, and let the rest of us become slaves to the lord of the land."

To increase the drama of the moment, the steward had been instructed to proceed with the search in order, beginning with the oldest brother first. As each sack was opened, and nothing unlawful was found, they must have breathed a sigh of relieve. But, then, when Benjamin's sack was opened, they must have been horrified. There was the missing chalice in his sack!

The brothers panicked. They tore their robes in anguish. What could they do? They could not allow anything to happen to Benjamin. He could not be put to death. The thought of telling Jacob that his beloved Benjamin was dead only served to remind them of the day they had returned with Joseph's bloody coat. They knew Jacob would not be able to survive another such tragedy. And they didn't think they could either. In a state of disbelief over the import of these events, the defeated brothers returned to Egypt.

God Has Found Us

This turn of events was serious indeed, and the brothers greatly mourned. Expecting his steward to arrive soon, Joseph had remained home. He was waiting for the group at his house. When they came into his presence, immediately they all fell before him and began to plead for mercy.

"What have you done?" Joseph demanded of them. "Didn't you consider that I might have divining powers?"

The brothers didn't know what to say. How could they possibly clear themselves? The evidence was there, and who could refute it?

Judah spoke for the whole group, he told Joseph that God was punishing them for some action they had all committed earlier in life. He then offered them all up as slaves.

"Oh, no," Joseph told them. "I require only that the man in whose sack the chalice was found be enslaved. The rest of you are free to return home."

It seems obvious this was Joseph's plan from the beginning. He wanted Benjamin with him in Egypt. When this was accomplished, he would send his brothers back to Canaan never to be seen again. He would then reveal himself to Benjamin, and they would live out their days together as a family. But the one thing Joseph had overlooked was the possibility that time and grief had changed his brothers.

People Change

When Joseph announced that the brothers were free to go with the exception of Benjamin, Judah became very bold. He could not permit this to happen. He could not and he would not return to Jacob without his Benjamin. He had to do something. He fearfully asked for permission to approach Joseph.

Granted this special concession, Judah began to plead his case before Joseph. He recounted their first trip to Egypt. He told him the story of their younger brother, Joseph, who had been eaten by wild animals. He told him that from the beginning they had known that it would be difficult to bring their younger brother because his father was so attached to him. He told Joseph of Jacob's great love for Joseph's brother, and how Jacob's life was bound up in Benjamin since the day of their brother Joseph's death. Jacob would not be able to bear the loss of the only remaining son of his beloved Rachel. Thus, Judah told Joseph the entire matter. "If we go back home without this lad," Judah declared, "our father will surely die."

God is the God of the second chance.

~

As he listened to Judah's genuine plea for Benjamin's life, Joseph remembered that it had been Judah who suggested to the other brothers that they sell him into slavery rather than kill him. Now this same Judah was pleading for the life of Benjamin.

God Is the God of the Second Chance

God is the God of the second chance. He had given Judah the opportunity to right the wrong of his past, and he seized it. In the same way, no matter what you've done, if you're willing, God will also give you the opportunity to make it right.

Something about Judah's painful plea caught Joseph off guard. He looked at Judah and then at his brothers. They were all in anguish over the thought of Benjamin being separated from the family. "I gave my father my word," Judah said. "I put myself up as a guarantee that I would bring Benjamin back safely." He begged Joseph to allow Benjamin to return with his brothers. He pleaded to be able to take Benjamin's place and live out his days in Egypt as Joseph's slave.

How this family had changed! The sight of Judah begging for Benjamin's life dispelled all of Joseph's former suspicions. He could see in that moment how much these men loved their father and how much they loved Benjamin. They were truly sorry for what they had done to him, and he could not bear to torment them any longer.

I Am Joseph

Joseph could take no more. He had wanted to see Benjamin and to know if the other brothers had been traumatizing him. He had wanted them to see what it felt like to be falsely accused and falsely imprisoned and not know when or if you would ever be free again. And he had wanted to see them powerless and squirming. He had accomplished his goals, but to his surprise he had not received any satisfaction from this fact.

Now, as Joseph listened to an obviously-changed Judah, something broke within him. God had done His work. He had allowed the wounds from Joseph's past to be reopened and cleansed. And in the process, God had replaced the pain with a softened, forgiving heart. Judah was not the only one who had changed; so had Joseph.

Joseph realized he still loved his brothers in spite of the way they had wronged him. He had tried to hold on to his revenge, but he could no longer do so. It was time to reveal his true identity to his brothers. He felt tears welling up inside of him, and he shouted for all of his servants to immediately leave the room. Then the floodgates of pain were released from the depths of his soul.

Joseph let out a piercing cry, and tears came rushing down his face. He bent over and wailed in agony. He cried and kept on crying. He cried loud, and he cried hard. He cried so loudly that *the Egyptians and the house of Pharaoh heard*" (Genesis 45:2). And as he cried, he let go of twenty-two years of pain.

The brothers were bewildered. They had no idea what was causing such an expression of grief in this Egyptian official. Finally, Joseph was able to control his sobs long enough to beckon them to come closer, and he whispered between sobs, *"I am Joseph; doth my father yet live?"* (Genesis 45:3).

The brothers just stood there dumbfounded. They were confused. Had they heard this man correctly? Did he say his name was Joseph? Why was he asking about their father? The man had spoken to them in their native tongue. They had no idea how to respond.

Joseph implored them to look closer, past the Egyptian garb and past his Egyptian looks. As they did so, with his strength gone from so much crying, Joseph quietly whispered, *"I am Joseph your brother, whom ye sold into Egypt"* (Genesis 45:4).

The brothers then looked into his eyes and saw him as he was. They had heard him correctly. The man before them was their little brother, their little brother they had thought so long to be dead. They were overjoyed. It was a miracle. As far as they were concerned, God had raised Joseph from the dead. What a wonderful scene that had to be!

Joseph then turned to Benjamin, fell upon his neck, hugged him and cried some more. All the brothers were now crying—Joseph, Benjamin, and the ten others as well.

Although the story doesn't say so specifically, I can imagine that Joseph then called for his wife and children and introduced them to his brothers. "This is Manasseh," I hear him saying: *'God hath made me to forget all my toil, and all my father's house.'* And this is Ephraim. *'God hath made me to be fruitful in the land of my affliction.'* " That had to be a very powerful moment.

CHAPTER 16

———⇒•◦•⇐———

The End of the Beginning

Getting their children successfully through the teen years is often a nightmare for parents. It seems that whatever they say is wrong. If the parent says, "Go right," the teenager seems to automatically tend to go left, and if the parent says, "Go left," the teenager always seems to want to go right. During these difficult years, teenagers often view their parents as being nosy, clueless as to what life is all about, and, in general, someone to avoid as much as possible.

When parents either forbid or put limits on phone calls, partying, drinking, drugs, and sex, all-out war often ensues. Often parents, realizing that these years will continue to present a series of lose-lose situations, then take a deep breath and pray that they will all make it through them alive.

But something happens between the ages of eighteen and twenty-one. The evil alien that has possessed their child for the past six to ten years now moves on, and the parents once again recognize their child. More amazingly, when that child has children of his or her own, the older their children get, the more your child hears your voice and your words coming out of their mouth.

Then one day, the whole thing comes to a head. As the now-grown man or woman walks down the hall, he or she happens to glance in the mirror. And when they do, they invariably scream. They have become their mother or father.

Someone once said, "Life is lived looking forward, but only understood looking backward." This is true of many facets of life. In the case of the now-grown teenager, when they have their own children, they come to understand the reasoning behind their parents' actions and words. They now clearly see why their parents allowed or, more often, did not allow them to participate in certain language, actions, attitudes, and friendships.

The same held true with Joseph. Before the arrival of his brothers in Egypt, his focus had been looking forward toward the future. But God was about to change that. He was about to give Joseph a lesson in looking back.

Open Mine Eyes

During the past months, Joseph had remembered times in his father's house, and with them, his dreams. As he had thought about this, at first, it seemed as if those dreams of long ago had been fulfilled. For years, countless people from Egypt and many other nations had bowed to him. However, in the dreams his father and brothers had been the ones bowing. This had not happened—until now.

With his brothers now bowing to him, Joseph wondered if there was a fuller meaning to the dreams. God had revealed to him the meaning of the butler's dream, the baker's dream and even Pharaoh's dream. Now he needed God to open his eyes and reveal to him the deeper meaning of his own dreams.

God is faithful, and we need but ask to receive. If Joseph would allow Him, God would open Joseph's eyes.

The End of the Beginning

The day Joseph revealed his identity ended up being the day he finally settled all of his issues with God, with his brothers, and with himself. That momentous day Joseph emptied his soul of any and all past pain, grief, and resentment. The tears he shed, however, did more than just cleanse his soul. Those tears also cleared his vision.

In the midst of his emotional release and his revelation to his brothers, God reminded him of why his brothers had come to Egypt. He suddenly realized that God had ordained this reunion with his family.

It all came together in that moment. God had foreknown this famine would take place on the earth. His brothers had come to Egypt in need of food, because the famine had reached Canaan. Without the provision of Egypt, the promised seed of Abraham would die. His father's bowing to him in the dream could only mean that Jacob would also eventually come to Egypt. It was now so clear. In His providential wisdom, God had chosen Joseph to go before his people and prepare a place for them.

In his dreams of long ago, God had shown Joseph *the end of the beginning*. The family of Jacob would leave Canaan and start over in Egypt.

The Place of Purpose

Joseph now realized that the events of that dreadful day when he had gone to Shechem in search of his brothers had been foreknown by God and ordained by God. When he had not been able to find his brothers, it would have been so easy to have turned around and gone home. He could have told his father that he had done his best to find his brothers, which would have been true. If Joseph had not gone those extra miles that day, he would not have met up with his brothers, and they could not have put into motion their murderous plot. But God had put a faithful spirit in Joseph, and so he had gone the extra mile. That good deed had led him to the pit.

God had also foreseen the anger of his brothers, and He hadn't stopped it. God had not intervened on purpose. Judah's plan to sell Joseph had actually come from God. His brother had planned to kill him, so God had sent the Ishmaelite slave traders to unknowingly save his life, and, in the process, provide him transportation to Egypt.

As dreadful as it all may have been, the pit had been God's place of purpose for Joseph. In that pit, Joseph realized for the first time that life would not be handed to him on a silver platter, that he could not entrust his future to other people, and that He had to know the Lord better. That pit had been Life 101 for Joseph. The Bible verses that tell of his experience there are quite short and lacking in detail, but we can be assured that God did a great work in Joseph, as he sat there terrified in that dark hole in the ground.

Walking behind a stinking camel over the sands of the desert toward Egypt was God's next place of purpose for Joseph. If he had thought, in those moments, that he would be required to do this for the rest of his life, baking in the hot sun and wearing his shoes out, he might have despaired. But this, too, was only for a season, and it was for a reason. That season would end when the reason was fulfilled.

The season for the caravan ended in Egypt. God's purpose had been fulfilled, and Joseph moved on to other things. We can be sure that if Joseph had brought a better price in some other city, his captors would have taken him there. But God wanted him in Egypt, so they were powerless to do anything else with him. He was right where God wanted him.

The slave market in Egypt was God's next place of purpose for Joseph. It represented humiliation, deprivation, and degradation, and yet God had a purpose in allowing His child to pass there. This, too, would not last forever. It was a momentary blip on the screen of destiny. Potiphar probably didn't know what had possessed him to buy the immature Hebrew, but he had little to do with it. God moved him, and he responded. Joseph had a lot to learn in his house. There he would take a class in Purpose 101.

So, the house of Potiphar was the next stop on Joseph's journey of purpose, and there it became apparent that God was with him. Everyone, even his master, could see it and appreciate it. Even though his stay in Potiphar's house ended in apparent tragedy, with Joseph being stripped once again and reduced to the state of a common prisoner, it was all part of God's plan.

Joseph had needed to go to Potiphar's house to learn something about administration, personnel management, agriculture, and many other things that would serve him well in the years to come. Now, as he sat in prison, he need not worry that he had somehow failed God. Just as he had needed to be in the house of Potiphar, he also needed to be in this prison. That's why God made all of the arrangements for his stay. This fact become clear when we see that there, in that prison, Joseph again prospered and rose to the top of the heap.

Even though the prison was God's next stop for Joseph, he may have been tempted to despair when it became apparent that his stay there would not be a short one, but he had learned at the other stops that no suffering is permanent and that if he kept it all in context, he would survive it. Paul later wrote to the Roman believers:

> *For I reckon that the sufferings of this present time are not worthy to be compared with the glory which shall be revealed in us.*

Romans 8:18

Joseph needed to be in that prison to learn about justice and injustice and about dealing with all classes of people. Once God elevated him over Egypt, he would need to be able to identify with more than those in the upper echelons of society. He would need to know how to identify with little people, the suffering ones, the disappointed ones, those whose hopes had been dashed.

God takes us through whatever training and stages are necessary to get us ready for what is ahead.

Finally, after Joseph had taken all of the necessary steps of purpose, and completed his journey, he was then able to step into his ultimate purpose and fulfill his destiny. But could he have jumped from his father's house to the palace? Never! Could Joseph have been successful as the prime minister of Egypt without first receiving the experience in Potiphar's house? Never! And could Joseph have ruled Egypt without the years of experience in the prison? Never! No, not in a million years! God knew just what He was doing at every step along the way.

Life Is Lived Looking Forward, But Only Understood Looking Backward

And so it is with each of us. We all have an ultimate destiny, a reason for living, and too often we would like to jump right into it without experiencing any pain, or trials, or tests, or deprivations of the flesh whatsoever. But it simply doesn't happen that way. God takes us through whatever training and stages are necessary to get us ready for what is ahead.

We are prone to despise these steps and treat them as detours to be avoided and escaped from as quickly and with as little effort as possible, but God knows the time we need to be at that particular stop in life. He alone controls the shuttle. And so, for each of you today, please know that you're in your purpose as much as you're on your way to your purpose.

Joseph was destined to become a savior to many, and that was a very noble purpose. Still, the journey to get there was important. And, along the way, during the process of purpose, he blessed a lot of people.

Money Can't Buy a Good Night's Sleep

God is an awesome God. If we let Him, He'll enable us to experience awesome forgiveness. Joseph's moment of revelation ended up being just as wonderful for the other brothers as it was for him. That day, after much kissing and crying, he told them:

> *Do not be angry with yourselves for selling me here, because it was to save lives that God sent me ahead of you. For two years now there has been famine in the land, and for the next five years, there will be no plowing nor reaping. But God sent me ahead of you to preserve for you a remnant on earth and to save your lives by a great deliverance.*
>
> Genesis 45:5-7, My Paraphrase

With Joseph now completely cleansed, he knew that even as this revelation had helped him, it would also help his brothers. He didn't want anything to spoil their reunion, and so even as he had let go of his pain, he felt it was now time for them to let go of their guilt. God had been gracious to all of them.

With those words, the heavy load of guilt his brothers had carried for so long was now lifted. Even though their deed had brought them twenty pieces of silver, when they experienced the consequences of that deed, they became subjected to continual mental bouts of torture. After so many years, they could now stop tormenting themselves over what they had done to their little brother. They could sleep well for the first time in more than twenty years.

What's Done in the Dark

God had foreseen the day when His people would be in physical need, and He had provided for that need in this unusual and wonderful way. He had also foreseen the need of their actually moving to Egypt for a time, and, through Joseph, He had provided a welcome for them there.

After seeing Joseph's cries of anguish turn to tears of joy, the whole house of Pharaoh rejoiced. Although Joseph was their beloved and respected leader, nevertheless he was a Hebrew. As we have seen, Egyptian law forbade them to even sit beside him as they are their meals. Because of that, at any given meal, Joseph sat apart from Asenath, Manasseh, and Ephraim and ate in isolation. Thus, they were all glad that Joseph's family had now come to Egypt.

When Pharaoh heard the wonderful news, he suggested that Joseph's brothers return to Canaan and bring Jacob and the whole family to live in Egypt. God was still working to honor his covenant with Abraham. So Joseph sent his brothers away once more, but this time, filled with joy and anticipation of his father's arrival.

He wisely told his brothers not to argue during the journey back to Canaan and well so. Even with all the joy of the reunion, they knew they would now have to face their father for what they had done so many years before.

People must come to realize the truth of the scripture:

Be not deceived; God is not mocked: for whatsoever a man soweth, that shall he also reap.

Galatians 6:7

This reaping may not come immediately, but sooner or later, it will materialize. Then, everything that has been done in the dark will come to the light.

The Walking Dead

Jacob had been anxiously watching the horizon each day, hoping for the return of his sons and his beloved Benjamin. Finally, one evening, there, in the distance, he saw their camels approaching.

When the brothers pulled up to his tent, they excitedly told him all that had happened on their trip to Egypt. At first Jacob, refused to believe their story. But then they presented the evidence. Jacob now noticed the empty wagons sent to transport the entire family to Egypt, and the cattle Joseph had sent

201

to Jacob, the brothers presented gifts that had been given to them, and finally Jacob began to consider the impossible. In that moment, something happened on the inside of him.

The day Joseph died Jacob also died. If Joseph's brothers thought that Jacob loved him too much while he was alive, they soon found that Jacob's love for his son was even greater in death. Jacob did not die physically that day, but a part of him died, and he began to mark time in life while he waited for death.

Death often does that. Death often strips us of our future. And it doesn't have to be physical death that leaves us in such a state. Although it can be the physical death of a loved one, it can also be the death of a relationship, the death of a friendship, the death of our health, the death of a career, or some other period in our lives, the death of hope, the death of a dream, or the death of anything that is dear to us. These can all leave us in a state of emptiness, while we mark time through life.

Even as a young child, I remember noticing that whenever the "old" men would retire from the steel mill, they seemed not to survive long afterward. After living for so many years, providing for their families and daily spending time with their "other family" in the mill, they were often now left so empty that they felt they no longer had a purpose for living.

People have to have some reason to get up in the morning. They have to have some reason to stay here on this earth and face all of the curves life throws their way. Those of you who are parents know that the reason many of us go on living is because of our children.

Children make life worth living, and our children are the reason we get up in the morning and we go to work in all types of weather. Our children are the reason we fight traffic, take flack on our jobs, and go to work even when we're not feeling well. Most women work two jobs: one away from home, and one at home—because of their children.

Many times, a parent can survive the death of a spouse, but the death of a child often leads to a string of other deaths—the marriage, friendships, and even the reason to go on living. Even the seeming loss of a child, as they grow up and leave home, often produces anxiety, now commonly called the "empty nest syndrome." When it comes, parents are left to figure out some reason to keep going.

We often stop living at such moments. No one buries us, and we still wake up every morning and go through the motions of life. But, in reality, we have become members of the society of the walking dead.

As for Jacob, with this news, the Bible tells us *"The spirit of Jacob their father revived"* (Genesis 45:27). Jacob had thought that his own death was imminent, but now he again had a reason for living. He would stay alive long enough to go to Egypt and see his beloved Joseph.

The Lion of the Tribe of Judah

The Bible is silent about how Jacob reacted to the revelation that his other sons had been complicit in Joseph's disappearance and that they had lied to him to cover up that fact. It does tell us that when you sow the wind you reap the whirlwind (see Hosea 8:7).

Jacob did not die soon after arriving in Egypt. He actually lived another seventeen years. But before he died, the brothers received their just due from him.

In Chapter 2, we discussed the fact that the birthright and blessing were passed on to the eldest son at his father's death. As was the custom, when Jacob was about to die (this time for real), he called his sons to him and prayed a blessing over each of them.

Even though Reuben was the eldest and should have gotten the double portion of the inheritance and been made lord of the family, Jacob didn't pass this honor on to him. He told Reuben that, although he was his firstborn, because of his weak character and his adultery with Jacob's concubine Bilhah, he would not receive the rights of the firstborn. He then told Simeon and Levi, the next two sons in the birth order, that this honor would also not be passed down to them, because of their cruelty to the Shechemites. (My audio tape on "The Consequence of Choice" records this entire incident for anyone wishing to know more about it).

God had already given Joseph the honor of being the present lord of the family, as his brothers now bowed to him, but the spiritual blessing of future lordship was given to Judah:

Judah, thou art he whom thy brethren shall praise .... Judah is a lion's whelp ... . The scepter shall not depart from Judah, nor a lawgiver from between his feet, until Shiloh come; and unto him shall the gathering of the people be.

Genesis 49:8-10

From the tribe of Judah would eventually come our beloved Savior Jesus Christ. The lion was the symbol of royalty in ancient days, the scepter was the symbol of power and dominion, and Shiloh was often used as a messianic term.

In this way, Jacob now passed down the spiritual blessing first given by God to his grandfather Abraham. Abraham had passed the blessing to Isaac, Isaac had passed it to Jacob, and Jacob now passed it to Judah. This kingship would eventually be passed to David, who came from the tribe of Judah, and eventually to the Messiah Himself, Jesus. This is why we refer to Jesus as *"the Lion of the tribe of Juda"* (Revelation 5:5) and as *"Jesus Christ, the son of David"* (Matthew 1:1).

As for passing down the material double portion of the inheritance, none of the other brothers was given that privilege either. I cannot help but think that this was due to their part in the malicious plot against Joseph. This honor was also given to him. Before Jacob called the twelve sons collectively to him, he had already called Joseph, along with his two sons to his bedside. At that time, Jacob formally adopted Joseph's sons, Manasseh and Ephraim. As adopted sons, each of them would receive a portion of Jacob's inheritance. Joseph, through his sons, would receive the birthright. Thus, Joseph was paid *double for his trouble* for his years of faithfulness to God, in light of immense suffering he had endured at the hands of wicked people and adverse circumstances.

Light + Dark = Twilight

As a final note to this wonderful account: as we have seen, had it not been for Joseph, the seed of Abraham would have starved to death in Canaan. But there was another reason, just as great, for Joseph's purpose in Egypt.

Isaac had faithfully carried the vision of his father Abraham, and Jacob had faithfully carried the vision of his father Isaac, but the sons of Jacob had not been faithful to the vision. Instead they were enticed toward heathen gods. Their association with the Canaanites was morally overcoming them. And they had begun to intermarry with the heathen women of Canaan. Now they were in danger of having the religious and moral values of their pagan wives integrated into their families. As a result, the seed of Abraham was becoming morally and spiritually corrupted.

This was a very serious matter. The promised Messiah was to come from this family. What was at stake here was not just the fate of a family, but also the fate of the whole world. God had spoken to Abraham, to Isaac, and Jacob to form the holy nation from which the promised Messiah could emerge. If that nation was corrupted and left the true faith, how could the Savior come?

Therefore, Israel was taken to Egypt, not just for physical preservation in time of famine, but for moral and spiritual preservation as well. The isolation of Goshen was needed to save the family from further corruption, and there the family grew to become a God-fearing nation. When the people of Israel eventually returned to Canaan, they were stronger for it.

God is the God of covenant. He had made a promise to Abraham, and He would keep that promise. God knew better than any man the physical perishing that existed during the famine was just symbolic of the more serious moral and spiritual problem of the family. They needed to get away to a place where they could be alone and there develop from the family of Jacob into the nation of Israel.

That's exactly what happened in Goshen. Seventy souls came out of Canaan to live in Egypt, but four hundred years later, when Moses led the people forth, they numbered several million.

In Goshen, the twelve brothers and their wives and children would develop into twelve tribes, and it was these tribes that would repopulate Canaan, the Promised Land.

CHAPTER 17

God's in Control

And we know that all things work together for good to them that love God, to them who are the called according to his purpose.

Romans 8:28

Faithfulness in Every Detail

We've now covered most of what we know about Joseph, so let me encourage you with these last thoughts. First, Joseph never left Egypt. He died there at one hundred and ten years old. Yet, though he never left the land of his affliction, he prospered there. The Bible tells us that God blessed him to see his children and grandchildren and great grandchildren before he died.

You, too, may never leave Egypt. I wish I could tell you differently, but God may have purpose for you in Egypt. If that is the case, God will bless you in Egypt—if you remain faithful to Him.

God gives this encouragement in Isaiah. If he chooses not to take you out of your wilderness situation, He will make a way for you right there *in* the wilderness. And if He chooses not to take you out of your desert, He will provide for you a river *in* the desert.

Throughout his life, Joseph consistently demonstrated this faithfulness. You can be sure that he was also a faithful husband, a faithful father, a faithful grandfather, a faithful uncle, and a faithful friend to those around him.

Faithfulness has to start somewhere. You may think that you would make a great leader, but have you been faithful to your friends and loved ones? Have you been faithful in business? Are you the last one to arrive at work in the morning and the first one to clock out? In spite of your poor job performance, do you now have a bad attitude because you don't understand why you've been passed over for promotion?

Have you been faithful in your role as a husband, wife, student, friend, etc.? Have you been faithful in the little things that bring no notice or reward?

As we look at Joseph, we see that he did not just face one test in life; he faced a whole series of tests. He did not just face one wrongdoer; he faced many. Yet, with each of his tests he was faithful. And because he was faithful, God moved him higher.

Joseph went from his father's house, to the pit, to the house of Potiphar, to the prison, and finally to the palace. With each step, he maintained his faithfulness. From this, God knew that He could trust Joseph to remain a faithful steward to Pharaoh and to the world at large.

Discovering Your Purpose in Life

I can't tell you what your specific purpose is in life, but I can tell you that, like Joseph, are very special to God. You're not like others. Somehow you're different, and you've been different your whole life. You've never looked at life in quite the same way as your siblings or your friends, and you never felt comfortable doing what they did—even when you were convinced to join them.

It hasn't always felt good to be different, and you may have wondered at times why it was so and how you could change it. But you can't. You're unique. God separated you from the time you were a small child for your specific purpose. What you've gone through and what you're going through right now is His way of preparing you for that purpose.

Somewhere, great purpose awaits you. When you finally step into it, you'll know that it has been nothing but the grace of God manifested in your life.

God Meant This Trial to Last For a Season, But You Made It a Lifestyle

In order to prepare for your great future, I urge you to let go of the past. Stop blaming people for what has happened, and start thanking God for it. He will use every negative thing that has ever come to your life for His glory. It's all been for a purpose.

Pain is a part of life, but if we don't approach it in the right way, the pain we suffer as a result of life's trials can leave us battle-scarred, weary, and sick. The sad truth is that many people, rather than rise to the occasion, allow what should have been a mere trial, to destroy their spirit and their faith. They become angry with God and men, and that anger eventually robs them of their fruitfulness. God only meant the trial to last for a season, but **they** made it a lifestyle.

There comes a time in life when we can no longer afford to focus on the wrong people have done to us or the people themselves who have done the wrong. We have to put it all behind us if we expect to move forward.

Nothing we can do will change the past. Our friends (or spouses or associates) have done what they've done, and we were powerless to prevent it. Will we now drown in self-pity or will we, rather, choose to move on? We can spend endless hours pondering what and who and why and what if, or we can forgive and forget and boldly face the new day that is upon us. If we insist on living our lives in the realm of "what if" and "if only," life will simply pass us by.

Hold on to Your Dream

We make choices to move on. That is my encouragement to you. With the truths you have seen in this book, I pray that you will now move past the past and into your future and purpose.

Whatever you do, hold on to your dream. Your purpose is wrapped in your dream, so don't let go of that dream for any reason. Get it before your eyes, and keep it before your eyes. Allow it to become the guiding factor, as you pass through any more periods of preparation. As I have said before, if you have allowed your dream to die, it's time to resurrect it.

Don't allow time or the drudgery of everyday life to rob you of your dream. Don't allow circumstances to rob you of your dream. Don't allow people to rob you of your dream. And don't allow problems to rob you of your dream.

All of these are nothing more than stepping-stones to the fulfillment of your dream. If God has permitted them to cross your path, then He has a reason for it. That reason is never for your destruction or discouragement. It is always for your betterment as a person.

The Birth of Ministry

Many of us have been angry with God for allowing things to happen to us. We're His children, so how could He do that? Joseph's story shows us just what the intent of a loving God is. He wants to see you in the palace, and whatever you need to face to get there is what He wants to send your way.

Joseph's story shows us just what the intent of a loving God is.

I urge you to resolve any issues you have with God because, deep down, it's really Him that you're blaming. We often feel that God could have stopped matters at any time He chose. He could have prevented it from happening this way, if He had wanted to. Just one word from Him, and things would have turned out very differently. So God, we think, is to blame.

So why didn't God intervene? We don't always know the answer to this question, but if we know that God chose not to intervene, that must mean that He had a good purpose in mind. Therefore, we can leave the decisions with Him, knowing that His ways are high above our ways:

For my thoughts are not your thoughts, neither are your ways my ways, saith the Lord. For as the heavens are higher than the earth, so are my ways higher than your ways, and my thoughts than your thoughts.

Isaiah 55:8-9

"Why would God allow anyone to be molested?" some might ask. What we fail to see is that perhaps, through this experience, as wrong and as painful as it was, they can have a future ministry to others who have also been molested. This is another reason that it is so important for people to allow God to heal them. Once they are healed, they can then bring healing to others.

As an example, the organization MADD (Mothers Against Drunk Drivers) was birthed from the pain of mothers losing children to irresponsible drunken drivers. Although God did not cause the tragedies, He allowed them to happen. But those mothers chose to move beyond their pain. They joined together and focused their energies outward and not inward. These women (and men) are fulfilling their purpose, and because of this, they have made the world a safer place.

In my upcoming book, *If God Loves Me So Much, Where Is He?* I will delve much deeper into this subject.

Resolving Your Issues with God

If you have issues you need to resolve with God, I urge you to pray and tell Him exactly what's on your heart. I promise you that He will hear you. I also promise you that if you'll allow Him to do so, He'll minister to your soul.

The reason you're reading this book is because God ordained it to be so. He ordained me to write this word of encouragement to you, and He ordained you to receive it.

After you pray, then ask God: "Lord, show me Your ways, and show me Your thoughts. Open the eyes of my understanding. Lord, open my eyes so that I might see You, open my ears so that I might hear You, and open my heart so that I might receive everything You have for me this day." Then leave the rest with God.

I encourage you to declare to yourself the truth that Joseph discovered so long ago: *"You meant evil against me, but God meant it for good"* (Genesis 50:20, NKJ). Now believe it, rejoice in it, and let it work in you. The past is past, and you cannot go back and change it. What you can do is to make the most of each moment you still have left on earth.

What you can do is tell Satan: "I refuse to allow this thing to hold me down, and I will not permit you to keep me in bondage any longer. I have chosen to be a forgiver because God is a forgiver. And I will continue to praise my God no matter what!"

For the many who have dreams that have not yet been fulfilled, please realize that as long as there is breath in your body, God still has purpose for you.

Finally, if you need to, have one last cry. Get all of those things out, and then put them behind you as quickly as possible. There's too much ahead of you for you to waste time focusing on pity and the past. Let it go once and for all.

Seasons of Testing

Despite all that you do to strengthen yourself spiritually, don't expect the seasons of testing to stop. We all go through them regularly. Each time we're about to move to a new level, a serious test will come. In some cases, hell is warring against God's purpose for us. But this only shows us that God uses hell's actions as a means of testing us. He allows the forces of hell to bring certain trials and cause delays so that we can prove ourselves faithful and strong. Paul wrote:

There hath no temptation taken you but such as is common to man: but God is faithful, who will not suffer you to be tempted above that ye are able; but will with the temptation also make a way to escape, that ye may be able to bear it.

1 Corinthians 10:13

The temptations we face in life, the trials of life, the many situations we face on a regular basis are only tests along the way that God has permitted as an opportunity for us to prove that we're ready to move on to greater things.

I challenge you to look back over your life and to be truthful in answering this question: When did you grow the most, when things were going well for you, or in times of pain? When did your character benefit the most, when things came easily for you, or when you have to persevere to get what you needed?

That's what worries me about a generation that's growing up right now thinking that someone owes them something and wanting everything handed to them on a silver platter.

In closing this important chapter, let me say that I would not want to leave a wrong impression. Although life holds much suffering, life is not all suffering in any sense of the word. It is only as we refuse to let go of our hurts that they follow us for years to come.

You will be called upon periodically to suffer, but when that suffering has run its course, get on with life. Go forward with new purpose. You have been prepared for something great. Now accomplish it without looking back. God has used every one of your trials to prepare you to accomplish His will. Now go forth and do it.

Bringing the Knowledge to Your World

Part of Joseph's purpose in Egypt was to bring the knowledge of God to those who lived there, and he did that through his consistently holy life, his service to others, and his willingness to speak openly of his faith. There is no evidence of Joseph ever being ashamed of God, whether he was standing before a fellow slave or before the mighty Pharaoh himself.

Ask God to reveal your purpose, and then let Him use you to change the world around you.

Part of your purpose in life is to bring the knowledge of God to those around you: your friends, your enemies, your coworkers, the heathen in your family, and the heathen on your job.

Ask God to reveal your purpose, and then let Him use you to change the world around you. He has placed you in a very specific place, surrounded by very specific people, under very specific circumstances—and all for His glory. If you will only be faithful where you are, you will be amazed to find that God will use you as a shining light.

The Sun Will Shine Tomorrow

As I close this chapter let me leave you with this final word of encouragement. Even with the setbacks and hardships life brings, we still live in a wonderful world. And life is still wonderful. This is true even for those of us who are Christians and look forward to the next world. Heaven will be wonderful, and being with Jesus will be so sweet, but none of us wants to be on the next train. We have a lot of living yet to do down here.

God paid Joseph double for his trouble, and in his latter years, Joseph's blessings far outweighed his sufferings. God can do this same thing for you.

I've said before that you need to make up your mind in the midst of the trial what your testimony will be when you come out of it ... because one day you will come out. Then life will seem brighter. Always remember that no matter how dark it may get, the sun will shine tomorrow.

Don't just exist. Learn to experience life, and experience it to the fullest. Your life is before you. But you have to make a choice to live it.

The Power of the Word

One of the things that can enable you to live life to the fullest and overcome any test or trial that might come your way is to fill yourself with the Word of God. Feast on it every day. That doesn't mean that you have to read the Bible all day long. Read it as much as you can, but also get some good teaching tapes, and listen to anointed preaching and teaching of the Word as you're able.

After most of my public messages, while encouraging people to invest in themselves with the ministry of audio tapes, I tell them that there was a time in life when I had been knocked down by many trials. But because the Word of God matures us and gives us understanding of Him, I didn't stay down long. You're only a baby once, but you can choose to stay in the crib all your life. Because of my dependence on God's Word, I no longer sit in a crib waiting for someone to feed me. I have learned to feed myself. I'm a big girl now.

Many ask me what Bible they should read. I have many Bibles of different versions. I grew up on the King James Version, so it's one of my favorites. But I also study the New King James Version, the New International Version, the New American Standard Version, and I love the *Everyday Bible* for younger believers and teens (the New Century Version). Get more than one version and compare them, and that way, you can gain the richness of the depth of meaning in God's Word.

I not only read the Bible; I go to hear other people teach it. If we are to teach, we first have to receive. When we teach, teach, and teach some more, there comes a time when we need to be refilled. This may be the reason that some seem to be able to give out the Word, but not to live it. They discover something in the Bible, and immediately they want to teach it to others—before even proving it in their own lives.

Be faithful in the Word and you will find that it has the power to keep you through everything that life may throw your way.

CHAPTER 18

The Fourth Man

I've often heard people say that Jesus is only to be found in the New Testament, but nothing could be further from the truth. The Old and the New Testaments record the history of God's people, from the beginning in Genesis to the end in Revelation. Genesis tells us how everything began, and Revelation tells us how it will end. It is a wise person who will see that history is in reality His Story.

The Fourth Man

If you really study the Old Testament, you will see that you cannot help but see Jesus there, whether as the Preincarnate Christ, or in shadows. In the book of Daniel, when King Nebuchadnezzar cast Shadrach, Meshach, and Abednego into the fiery furnace, the king himself acknowledged that there was another person walking around in the fire with them:

Then Nebuchadnezzar the king was astonied, and rose up in haste, and spake, and said unto his counsellers, Did we not cast three men bound into the midst of the fire? Lo, four men loose, walking in the midst of the fire, and they have no hurt; and the form of the fourth is like the Son of God!

Daniel 3:24-25

That fourth man was Jesus, and even the heathen king Nebuchadnezzar recognized it. Whether it is in the account of God calling Gideon (Judges 6) or in His bringing Samson's mother the news of her upcoming delivery (Judges 13), the Preincarnate Jesus is there.

Four hundred years after Jacob brought his family to Egypt, God raised up Moses to lead them back to Canaan. During their forty years of wandering in the desert, God instructed Moses to build the Tabernacle, which provides a fascinating study in the Godhead—Father, Son, and Holy Ghost.

At the end of this period, Joshua took the leadership of God's people. When he led the people across the Jordan River, we see a picture of the salvation Jesus provides believers. When he sent the spies to Rahab's house, we see a picture of Jesus. And when God led them to the strongest citadel in Canaan, Jericho, we again see Jesus:

So the people shouted when the priests blew with the trumpets: and it came to pass, when the people heard the sound of the trumpet, that the people shouted with a great shout, that the wall fell down flat.

Joshua 6:20

For the Lord himself shall descend from heaven with a shout, with the voice of the archangel, and with the trump of God: and the dead in Christ shall rise first: Then we which are alive and remain shall be caught up together with them in the clouds, to meet the Lord in the air: and so shall we ever be with the Lord.

1 Thessalonians 4:16-17

The story of Joseph is filled with such pictures and shadows. Allow me the privilege of giving you some of these:

1. Joseph was loved by his father Jacob, and when John the Baptist baptized Jesus, God the Father spoke from heaven and said, *"This is my beloved Son, in whom I am well pleased"* (Matthew 3:17).

2. Joseph was hated by his brothers, and Jesus was hated in the same way. He said, *"If the world hate you, ye know that it hated me before it hated you"* (John 15:18).

3. Joseph was rejected by his brothers, and Jesus told His disciples, *"The Son of man must suffer many things, and be rejected of the elders and chief priests and scribes, and be slain, and be raised the third day"* (Luke 9:22). To this day, many of His Jewish brothers still reject Him.

4. Joseph was sent by his father to his brothers, and Jesus was sent by His Father into the world. *"But when the fullness of the time was come, God sent forth his Son, made of a woman"* (Galatians 4:4).

5. Joseph's brothers conspired to kill him, and the Bible says of the chief priests and Pharisees: *"Then from that day forth they took counsel together for to put him to death"* (John 11:53).

6. Joseph was stripped of his coat by his brothers, and when Jesus was on trial before Pilate, although Pilate proclaimed Him to be innocent, He was taken into the common hall and stripped: *"And they stripped him"* (Matthew 27:28).

7. Joseph was sold for twenty pieces of silver, and when Judas agreed to betray Jesus, the chief priests agreed to pay him a slightly larger sum: *"thirty pieces of silver"* (Matthew 26:15).

8. Joseph was tempted by Potiphar's wife, yet he chose not to sin. The Bible tells us Jesus identifies with us in our sufferings because He, too, *"was in all points tempted like as we are, yet without sin"* (Hebrews 4:15).

9. Joseph was thirty when he finally stood before Pharaoh and stepped into his purpose. Jesus was a similar age when He began His earthly ministry: *"And Jesus himself began to be about thirty year of age"* (Luke 3:23).

10. Joseph's Egyptian name, Zaphnath-paaneah, meant "savior," and the name Jesus means "Jehovah saves."

11. Joseph suffered greatly for purpose, and Jesus suffered the death on the cross for our salvation.

12. Joseph was given a Gentile bride; Asenath, and we Christians are called the Bride of Christ.

13. Joseph's brothers didn't recognize him because of the Egyptian clothing he was wearing. Men and women of the first century failed to recognize Jesus because He had taken on the form of man and clothed himself with humanity.

14. Although Joseph was in Egypt, he was never one of the Egyptians. Jesus, too, said, *"I am not of the world."* (John 17:14).

15. Joseph had to go to Egypt to keep his people from perishing, and the Bible tells us of Jesus: *"God so loved the world, that he gave his only begotten Son, that whosoever believeth in him should not perish, but have everlasting life"* (John 3:16).

16. Joseph went ahead of his family to prepare a place for them in Egypt, and before He ascended to heaven, Jesus said, *"In my Father's house are many mansions: if it were not so, I would have told you. I go to prepare a place for you"* (John 14:2).

17. Joseph didn't just save his family from perishing; he saved many other people from many other nations. Jesus didn't just come to save the house of Israel; He came to save all mankind.

18. Joseph went down into the pit (the earth), and during the three days Jesus was in the grave, He went down into hell, defeated Satan, and took away *"the keys of hell and of death"* (Revelation 1:18). Jesus then victoriously paraded the enemy through the corridors of hell: *"And having spoiled principalities and powers, he made a shew of them openly, triumphing over them in it"* (Colossians 2:15). During ancient times, when wars were over, the conquering commander would lead his armies through town proclaiming victory. The defeated army, stripped, would follow behind the victorious general.

19. Joseph appeared to his brothers after they had thought he was dead, and Jesus rose from the dead and appeared to many after men thought He, too, was dead. *"That Christ died for our sins according to the scriptures; and that he was buried, and that he rose again the third day according to the scriptures: And that he was seen of Cephas [Peter], then of the twelve: After that, he was seen of above five hundred brethren at once"* (1 Corinthians 15:3-6).

20. Joseph was eventually exalted, and all of the then-known world bowed to him. The Bible tells us the day will come when *"at the name of Jesus every knee should bow … And that every tongue should confess that Jesus Christ is Lord, to the glory of God the Father"* (Philippians 2:10-11).

21. Joseph suffered a painful separation from his father to save his fellow man, and Jesus also suffered a painful separation from His Father to save the whole world. On the cross, He cried, *"My God, my God, why hast thou forsaken me?"* (Mark 15:34).

These are just some of the many ways Joseph appears to us as a shadow of Christ. As I said, if you will just open your eyes and look, you can see Him in every book of the Bible and at every turn of events, Old and New Testaments alike.

Your Purpose Is Bigger Than You, and It's About More Than You

You have been placed on this earth to make a difference to mankind. That might be a little overwhelming, but it's true.

The purpose of this book has been to encourage you on your journey of purpose. But purpose without Jesus is no purpose at all. It's just someone doing what they want to do for their own glory. When this happens, the success the person achieves does not bring with it the promised joy, satisfaction, or peace. And the money that is acquired often is accompanied by great heartache.

You have been placed on this earth to make a difference to mankind.

One of the many things I admire about Oprah Winfrey is her great love of giving. She was always Oprah, but she was not always OPRAH. Now that she is, she has not forgotten the "little" people. All of this, in spite of her sufferings, which have been many. (Remember, with great purpose comes suffering, and Oprah is no different.) Still, she chooses to give, and because of this attitude of giving, the fame and fortune she has acquired mean all the more.

It's not Oprah Winfrey's fame that has made the difference in her life, but rather what she has done with that fame. I guarantee that if she were not the giver she is, she would never have received the satisfaction her career now brings to her.

As a side note: you might say to yourself, "If I had her money, I could give too." But allow me to ask you: are you giving away some of the money you make? And for those of you who think, "If I have to suffer, I'd rather do it in luxury" you need to know that this is a foolish statement, as if the surroundings of someone truly experiencing the depths of despair can make a difference.

Rich and poor people alike both commit suicide. Rich and poor people both get divorced. Rich and poor people both can become devastated in life. In most of these cases, the people involved can't even see the surroundings because of the painful experiences they're enduring.

You Cast the Deciding Vote

As you have read this book, I'm sure you've been able to picture the events of Joseph's life, and I now want to leave you with one more picture.

As my sons were growing up, our home was "the community home." Most know what I am talking about when I use this phrase. Our home was always full of hungry teenagers. On Saturday morning, I would look over our balcony to see how many of them had spent the night sleeping on the family room floor.

During those years, I did a lot of witnessing and ministering to the kids who came our way. Sometimes this was done verbally, sometimes it was done through our lifestyle, and sometime it was done with displays. As far as I was concerned, these were my students, so I would type verses and tape them onto areas where they congregated, especially in the kitchen.

On my kitchen cabinets, I displayed many messages prepared on my computer. One of these was placed on three pieces of paper and taped onto three cabinets. It said:

For God so loved the world, that he gave his only begotten Son, that whosoever believeth in him should not perish, but have everlasting life.

John 3:16

One of my personal favorites was the empty frame that I hung at the bottom of the staircase. A sign extending from it said, *"A life without Jesus is an empty life."* If you've never accepted Jesus as your Savior and Lord, you, too, are living an empty life. You're living life on your own and without Jesus. I guarantee that life will be hard for you. And you're missing out on so much. Most importantly, you're missing out on the purpose God created you for.

The Bible tells us:

The fool has said in his heart, "There is no God"

Psalm 14:1, NKJ

It takes a very foolish person to not be able to look around and see that *Somebody made all of this.* If you are in that group, I strongly encourage you to take a week or so and watch the Discovery Channel. As you watch amazing accounts of the animal kingdom, the plant kingdom, the birds of the air, the abundant life in the oceans of the world, or the stars in the sky, you will come to realize that *all this didn't just happen.*

Some of you need no more convincing. God has spoken to your heart, and you simply want to know how you can make the God of Joseph your God. You should know that Jesus came and died on the cross for you. He wants you to invite Him into your heart, so that He can guide you into truth and purpose, and have you come to heaven when you die.

Satan, on the other hand, also wants your company with him—in hell. He does all in his power to keep people from accepting Jesus.

This is how I say it while ministering. *Jesus has cast a vote for your eternal soul, and Satan has cast a vote for your eternal soul. Now, you cast the deciding vote.* It's your choice.

People have the tendency to believe that a loving God would not send anyone to hell. They're absolutely right. God never sends anyone to hell. People send themselves to hell because they don't freely receive that which has been freely given.

What about you? Would you like to accept the Lord Jesus Christ as your personal Lord and Savior? Responding to God is a sign of humility and the recognition that no one can help you but Jesus. God honors the humble heart, and He will hear your cry.

As you pray today, surrender to the Lord all of your hurts, all of your pains, all of your griefs, and all of your heavy burdens. Give it all to Him.

Today is your day of salvation. Today is your day of deliverance. Today is the day when the power of sin will be broken in your life.

Jesus tells us:

Behold, I stand at the door, and knock: if any man hear my voice, and open the door, I will come in to him, and will sup with him, and he with me.

Revelation 3:20

Ask yourself this question: If you died today, would you go to heaven? If you're not sure of the answer, then you need to pray and ask Jesus to come into your heart.

Jesus is standing knocking at the door of your heart right now. He wants to come in. But the only doorknob is the one on the inside. You have to open it yourself. He will not force His way into your life. He has given us free will, so we have a choice.

You may be a churchgoer. You may have been in church five, ten, or even twenty years, but you're still not sure if you're on your way to heaven. Whatever the case, whether you need to invite Jesus into your heart for the first time. or if you need reassurance of your salvation, I invite you to pray with me now:

Lord Jesus,

I need You. I open the door of my life and receive You as my Savior and Lord. Jesus, thank You for dying for me. I ask that You would forgive me of my sins. Lord Jesus, please come into my heart. Take control of my life. And make me the kind of person you want me to be.

Amen!

Once we invite Jesus into our hearts, we never have to do this again. Jesus assures us in His Word that He will never leave or forsake us:

For he hath said, I will never leave thee nor forsake thee.

Hebrews 13:5

Others may forsake us, but Jesus will be there for us—no matter what. If we turn our back on Him, He's always near, waiting for us to confess that which has separated us from Him. And, when we do, He brings us back into fellowship with Him.

This may be where you are right now. You know that you have received the Lord into your heart in the past, but due to sin, apathy, or disillusionment, you have slipped away. You now would like to restore your relationship with Jesus. I encourage you to pray too. You may be thinking, "I don't deserve to be saved. You don't know the horrible things I've said and done. Jesus will never forgive me."

Well, you're right about being undeserving of salvation. But the truth is that none of us deserves salvation. God tells us that in His word. No, God offers us salvation out of His divine love and purpose for us. No one deserves it, no one can buy it, and no one can earn it. God fixed it that way so that we could not take any credit for our salvation. It's all from Him.

As far as the terrible things you did in the past, allow me end this book with one of my favorite stories.

Please Come Home

There was once a young girl named Maria. She and her mother Christina lived in a remote foreign village. Maria's father had died some years earlier, and the family was very poor. As Maria grew, she would often fall asleep as she watched the flickering lights coming from the big city. She would ask her mother, "Can we go to the city?" But Christina strictly forbade this.

Maria was fascinated with those lights, and as she grew, they only captivated her more and more. One day when Christina came home, she noticed that all of Maria's clothes were gone. Seeing the outline of the city in the distance, she knew instantly that Maria had gone there.

Christina was determined that she would go to the big city and bring her daughter home. And so, gathering the little money she had and borrowing the rest, Christina bought a bus ticket to the big city.

Before she left, Christina went to the only photographer in the village and asked that he take her picture. She had no money, but she asked him if, out of sympathy for her situation, he would make several copies of this picture. He agreed. Finally, with pictures and ticket in hand, Christina boarded the bus and went to the big city to find her Maria.

After inquiring for weeks, Christiana finally learned that Maria was indeed there in the town, but she was in bad shape. She had become a prostitute. Over the coming weeks, Christina visited all the houses of ill repute she could find in the area. At each one, she scribbled something on the back of her picture, and then hung it in the lobby where it could be seen.

She knew that what she was doing was dangerous, for she was going into unsafe neighborhoods and encountering rather terrifying people, but she refused to allow her fears to stop her. She was determined to find her daughter.

One morning, after spending a very hard night, Maria stumbled down the steps of one of the houses of prostitution. In the distance, she thought she caught sight of a familiar face. The hallway was dimly lit, but as she slowly entered the lobby, there on the wall was a picture of her mother.

She couldn't believe it. Thoughts of home flooded her mind. Oh how she missed Christina. Oh how Maria now wished she had listened to her mother. But it was too late now. Her life was a mess, and she was filled with shame. She knew that going home would only bring disgrace to her mother.

Tears welled up in Maria's eyes as she remembered happier days. As she held the photo, looking at it longingly, she turned it over and noticed that something was written on the back. There Maria read the words her mother had penned, hoping for just such a moment: *No matter where you've been, and no matter what you've done, I still love you. Please come home.*

And so I close with these final words: No matter how dark your past, you can have a spotless future. There's absolutely nothing that you may have done that God cannot forgive you of. He still loves you. He tells us in His Word that nothing can separate us from His love. He even enumerates some of the things He says cannot do it:

Neither death, nor life, nor angels, nor principalities, nor powers, nor things present, nor things to come, Nor height, nor depth, nor any other creature, shall be able to separate us from the love of God, which is in Christ Jesus our Lord.

Romans 8:38-39

I encourage you to pray:

Lord Jesus,

Forgive me for walking away from You. Forgive me for the horrible things I've said and done. Lord Jesus, I now come back to You. I thank You for Your forgiveness and ask that You give me the power to forgive myself. Lord, I now ask that You make it possible that somehow I can right the wrongs of my past.

Amen!

Now, you've done what God has required of you, and He has done what was required of Him. Therefore, it's done. Commit, from this day forward, to be like Joseph. You will remain faithful to God, whether in Egypt or wherever God allows you to go. You will not allow roots of bitterness from the actions of others to spring up in your heart, and, in this way, you will take control of your destiny—no matter what the cost.

Now, let Him be Lord in your life. He is El Roi, the God who sees all, Jehovah-Jireh, the Lord who provides, Jehovah-Rapha, the Lord who heals, Jehovah-Tsidkenu, the Lord our righteousness, Jehovah-Nissi, the Lord our banner, and Jehovah-Shammah, the Lord who is present. Most of all, He is Jehovah-Ra'ah, the Lord our Shepherd. He wants to be all of this and more to you—if you will let Him do it.

He came unto his own, and his own received him not. But as many as received him, to them gave he power to become the sons of God, even to them that believe on his name: Which were born, not of blood, nor of the will of the flesh, nor of the will of man, but of God.

John 1:11-13

And being found in fashion as a man, he humbled himself, and became obedient unto death, even the death of the cross. Wherefore God also hath highly exalted him, and given him a name which is above every name: That at the name of Jesus every knee should bow, of things in heaven, and things in earth, and things under the earth; And that every tongue should confess that Jesus Christ is Lord, to the glory of God the Father.

Philippians 2:8-11

And this is the record, that God hath given to us eternal life, and this life is in his Son. He that hath the Son hath life; and he that hath not the Son of God hath not life. These things have I written unto you that believe on the name of the Son of God; that ye may know that ye have eternal life, and that ye may believe on the name of the Son of God.

1 John 5:11-13